I0748864

TRANSACTIONS

of the

American Philosophical Society

Held at Philadelphia for Promoting Useful Knowledge

VOLUME 78, Part 5, 1988

The Oxford Collection of the Drawings of Roger de Gaignières and the Royal Tombs of Saint-Denis

ELIZABETH A. R. BROWN

Brooklyn College and The Graduate School,
City University of New York

THE AMERICAN PHILOSOPHICAL SOCIETY

Independence Square, Philadelphia

1988

Library of Congress Catalog
Card Number-87-72869
International Standard Book Number 0-87169-785-8
US ISSN 0065-9746

CONTENTS

DEDICATION

This study is dedicated, with affection and gratitude for their friendship, encouragement, and inspiration, to the late Robert Branner and to Shirley Prager Branner.

ACKNOWLEDGMENTS

One of the chief pleasures of research is the time spent pursuing evidence and discussing and refining ideas. I am grateful to the many people who have answered my queries, debated my hypotheses, suggested changes stylistic and substantive, and facilitated my access to countless books, manuscripts, documents, and works of art. I offer special thanks to Bruce Barker-Benfield of the Bodleian Library; the late Jean Adhémar; Françoise Bercé, conservator of the Archives et Bibliothèque de la Direction du Patrimoine; and Françoise Gardey, conservator of the Réserve des estampes of the Bibliothèque nationale. I also express my deep gratitude for advice and assistance to François Avril, Françoise Baron, Marie-Noëlle Baudouin-Matuszek, Robert-Henri Bautier, Shirley Prager Branner, Ralph Sawyer Brown, Jr., Madeline Harrison Caviness, William W. Clark, Michael W. Cothren, Richard C. Famiglietti, Jean-René Gaborit, Marie-Madeleine Gauthier, Paula Lieber Gerson, Christopher Hohler, Hervé Pinoteau, Michèle Prouté, Jane Rosenthal, Patricia Danz Stirnemann, Jean-Bernard de Vaivre, and Richard M. White. The Keeper of Western Manuscripts of the Bodleian Library has kindly permitted me to quote from various records of the Library; since the Bodleian's internal "Library Papers" are being reinventoried, the class marks which I give are temporary, but concordances of old and new class marks will be available when the rearrangement is completed. I appreciate as well the generous assistance of the staffs of the Archives nationales, Avery Architectural and Fine Arts Library and Butler Library of Columbia University, the Bibliothèque Mazarine, the Bibliothèque nationale, the Bodleian Library, the British Library, the Department of Prints and Drawings of the British Museum, the Fitzwilliam Museum, the Musée de l'Ile-de-France at Sceaux, the Musée national des Châteaux de Versailles et de Trianon, the New York Public Library, Sir John Soane's Museum and Architectural Library, and the Society of Antiquaries. The study would not have been possible without the financial support of the National Endowment for the Humanities, the American Council of Learned Societies, and the PSC-CUNY Research Award Program of the City University of New York, and the generous help of my colleagues at Brooklyn College. To them all I extend sincere thanks.

INTRODUCTION

In the late seventeenth and early eighteenth centuries, François-Roger de Gaignières (1642–1715) amassed an impressive collection of drawings of the tombs and other monuments of France.[1] That collection is today divided between the Bodleian Library in Oxford and the Bibliothèque nationale in Paris. It is ironic that such a fate should have befallen a collection gathered by a man dedicated to France's past, a man who devoted a good part of his life and fortune to preserving, through drawings and transcriptions, records of the monuments and documents of his own country.[2] Doubly ironic is the fact that the sixteen volumes of the

---

[1] Although my research began before the appearance of his catalogue, my work has been greatly facilitated by Jean Adhémar's publication of reproductions of the drawings of tombs executed for Roger de Gaignières: Jean Adhémar, with the collaboration of Gertrude Dordor et al., "Les tombeaux de la Collection Gaignières. Dessins d'archéologie du XVIIe siècle," *Gazette des Beaux-Arts* 116e année, 6e pér., 84 (July–September 1974); 118e année, 88 (July–August, September 1976); and 119e année, 90, (July–August 1977). Adhémar was unable to include in his collection reproductions of the drawings in the Oxford collection and published in their place copies of the tracings in the collection of the Réserve des estampes of the Bibliothèque nationale that will be discussed below. Adhémar's work has been continued by Jean-Bernard de Vaivre, in "Dessins inédits de tombes médiévales bourguignonnes de la Collection Gaignières," *Gazette des Beaux-Arts* 128e année, 6e pér., 108 (October 1986): 97–122, and ibid. (November 1986): 141–82; and idem, "Le fonds Gaignières," a paper delivered on 26 May 1988 at a conference at Fontevraud on "La figuration des morts dans la chrétienté médiévale jusqu'à la fin du premier quart du XIVe siècle," which will be published with the papers of the colloquium. See also idem, "Sur trois primitifs français du XIVe siècle et le portrait de Jean le Bon," in ibid., 123e année, 6e pér., 97 (April 1981): 131–56, and idem, "Les tombeaux des sires de Bourbon (XIIIe et première partie du XIVe siècles)," *Bulletin monumental* 138 (1980): 365–403. Adhémar ("Tombeaux" [1974]: 10, n. 7) drew attention to the similar enterprise of the Belgian Antoine de Succa (1567–1620). Succa's work has recently been comprehensively analyzed and illustrated in Micheline Comblen-Sonkes and Christiane Van Den Bergen-Pantens, *Mémoriaux d'Antoine de Succa, un contemporain de Rubens. Dessins du XVIIe siècle*, 2 vols. (Exposition organisée à la Bibliothèque royale Albert Ier; Publication du Centre National des Recherches Primitifs Flamands, III, Contributions à l'étude des primitifs flamands, 7; Brussels: Bibliothèque royale Albert Ier, 1977).

The following abbreviations will be used: ADP—Paris, Archives de la Direction du Patrimoine; AN—Paris, Archives nationales; Bodl.—Oxford, The Bodleian Library; BL—London, British Library; BM—London, British Museum; BN—Paris, Bibliothèque nationale; CRMH—Paris, Palais de Chaillot, Centre de Recherches sur les monuments historiques; GD-G—MS. Gough Drawings-Gaignières; RE—Réserve des estampes; SSDB—Seine-Saint-Denis-Basilique.

[2] Essential information regarding Roger de Gaignières and his collections is given in Michel Hennin, *Les monuments de l'histoire de France. Catalogue des productions de la sculpture, de la peinture et de la gravure, relatives à l'histoire de la France et des Français, 481–1610*, 10 vols. (Paris: C. Lahure, J. F. Delion, 1856–63), 1: 269–77; Léopold Delisle, *Le Cabinet des manuscrits de la Bibliothèque impériale. . . .* , 3 vols. (Histoire générale de Paris, Collection de documents

Gaignières collection now housed in Oxford include the drawings of the most prestigious French tombs, those of the members of the royal family interred at Saint-Denis. These are found in one volume. In the other fifteen are similar drawings of funerary monuments of Paris, the Ile-de-France, and northern and central France, as well as drawings, many of them colored, of tapestries, stained glass, and other precious objects. The Oxford volumes contain some 1900 drawings, a fourth of the surviving Gaignières drawings.

The history of the Gaignières collection and its dispersal is well known, but the curious circumstances under which the Oxford collection was rediscovered by the French in the mid-nineteenth century have never been explored. This story, inextricably involved with the history of the restoration and installation of royal tombs at the basilica of Saint-Denis by François Debret (1777–1850), Ferdinand, Baron de Guilhermy (1808–78), and Eugène Viollet-le-Duc (1814–79), is fully as complex as the history of the early fortunes of the collection itself.

The collection of Roger de Gaignières suffered its first major losses at the hands of Pierre de Clairambault (1651–1740), the royal genealogist who, nine years younger than Gaignières, outlived him by twenty-five years. Gaignières had pledged his entire collection to Louis XIV in 1711 in return for a life-time annuity. At his death the collection was transferred to the royal library, but in the process Clairambault managed to take for himself more than a hundred volumes. Added to his library, they eventually returned to the royal library with his own impressive collection.[3]

The volumes of the Gaignières collection spared by Clairambault were for a time preserved together at the royal library. They were used by such scholars as Bernard de Montfaucon, who, in the preface to his work on the

---

fondée avec l'approbation de l'Empereur par M. le Baron Haussmann, No. 10; Paris, Imprimerie impériale [nationale], 1868–81), 1: 335–56, 553–56; Henri-François-Xavier-Marie Bouchot, *Inventaire des dessins exécutés pour Roger de Gaignières et conservés aux Départements des estampes et des manuscrits,* 2 vols. (Paris: E. Plon, Nourrit, 1891), particularly the introduction to the first volume; Joseph Guibert, *Le Cabinet des estampes de la Bibliothèque nationale. Histoire des collections suivie d'un guide du chercheur* (Paris: Maurice le Garrec, 1926), 41–49; Louis-Jean Guenebault, "Notice sur la Collection Gaignières," *Revue archéologique* 10, part 1 (1853): 43–52; Georges Duplessis, "Roger de Gaignières et ses collections iconographiques," *Gazette des Beaux-Arts* 12e année, 2e pér., 3 (1870): 468–88; and Charles de Grandmaison, "Gaignières, ses correspondants et ses collections," *Bibliothèque de l'Ecole des Chartes* 51 (1890): 573–617, 52 (1891): 181–219, 53 (1892): 5–76. Joseph Guibert published a partial inventory, organized geographically, of the drawings of tombs, windows, and tapestries, but the usefulness of his volumes (which contain reproductions of the drawings) is limited by their incompleteness and by his failure to give the precise locations of the drawings: Joseph Guibert, *Les dessins d'archéologie de Roger de Gaignières, publiés sous les auspices et avec le concours de la Société de l'histoire de l'art français,* 15 vols. (13 in Série I, "Tombeaux"; 1 in Série II, "Vitraux"; and 1 in Série III, "Tapisseries"; no volumes of the projected Série IV, "Topographie," ever appeared) (Paris: Catala Frères, 1912–13).

[3] See Delisle, *Cabinet des manuscrits,* 2: 18–25; and Duplessis, "Gaignières," 481–82.

monuments of the French monarchy, gave pride of place in his acknowledgments to the collection of "son ami," Roger de Gaignières.[4] The Gaignières collection consisted of a variety of materials—transcriptions of documents, genealogical notes and records, depictions of seals, topographical drawings, and a series devoted to costumes, as well as drawings of funerary monuments and other works of art. Thus it is not surprising that, with the specialization and rationalization of the royal holdings that occurred in the eighteenth century, the collection was divided. At least in part as a result of the division, between 1779 and 1784 many drawings, most of which are now in the Bodleian Library, were removed from the royal library. Just how the drawings were taken is unclear, although Jean-Baptiste Guillaume de Gevigney, conservator of documents and genealogies at the royal library from 1779 to 1784, seems clearly to have stolen them.[5] Their large size and excellent state of preservation testify to the culprit's care and ingenuity. The stolen drawings may have been disposed of initially in France, where a number remained and eventually found their way back to the national library.[6] The major part, however—fourteen volumes and two portfolios—crossed the Channel to England, perhaps before, perhaps during the Revolution. In England they were acquired by Richard Gough (1735–1809). Since he served from 1771 to 1797 as director of the Society of Antiquaries, he was well placed to learn of the drawings' arrival. His passionate interest in things funerary explains his acquisition of the collection; between 1786 and 1789 he published a study of the sepulchral monuments of Great Britain which clearly reflects the influence

[4] Bernard de Montfaucon, *Les monumens de la monarchie françoise . . .* , 5 vols. (Paris: Julien-Michel Gandouin and Pierre-François Giffart, 1729–33), 1: vi; see also Guenebault, "Notice," 44; and Duplessis, "Gaignières," 486–87. Montfaucon's volumes of sketches and notes reveal the extent of his reliance on the Gaignières collection: see particularly BN, lat. 11913, nos. 7–8; lat. 11920, fols. 161–68; and fr. 15634–35 ("Dessins et gravures pour les Monuments de la monarchie françaїse"), in which most of the drawings are keyed to specific items in the collection. For other scholars who used the collection, see Bouchot, 1: iv–v; and Duplessis, "Gaignières," 473–77.

[5] On the reorganization of the library, see Delisle, *Cabinet des manuscrits,* 1: 553–54; and Duplessis, "Gaignières," 484. On the disappearance of the volumes, see Appendix III below.

[6] See Bouchot, 1: xxiii for Albert Lenoir's acquisition of the volume now catalogued as Pe 11 in BN, RE, which obtained it from Lenoir in 1883. In 1860 the Bibliothèque Mazarine had thirty-two drawings, subsequently deposited at the Bibliothèque nationale: Dauban, "Rapport adressé à Son Excellence M. le Ministre de l'Instruction publique et des cultes, au nom de la Section d'archéologie du Comité des travaux historiques, au sujet de la collection Gaignières d'Oxford," *Revue des Sociétés savantes des départements* 2nd ser., 4 (1860): 174, n. 2. In 1840 the volumes now catalogued as Pe 11b–11c were transferred from the Cabinet des manuscrits to the Cabinet des estampes: Bouchot, xxiii. According to Bouchot, the Cabinet des estampes now possesses 4273 of the Gaignières drawings, the Cabinet des manuscrits 678, and the Bodleian Library 1844. To these must be added the 248 drawings in the Cabinet des manuscrits found by de Vaivre: "Dessins inédits," passim. As de Vaivre points out (ibid., 97), other drawings may well be found in the future.

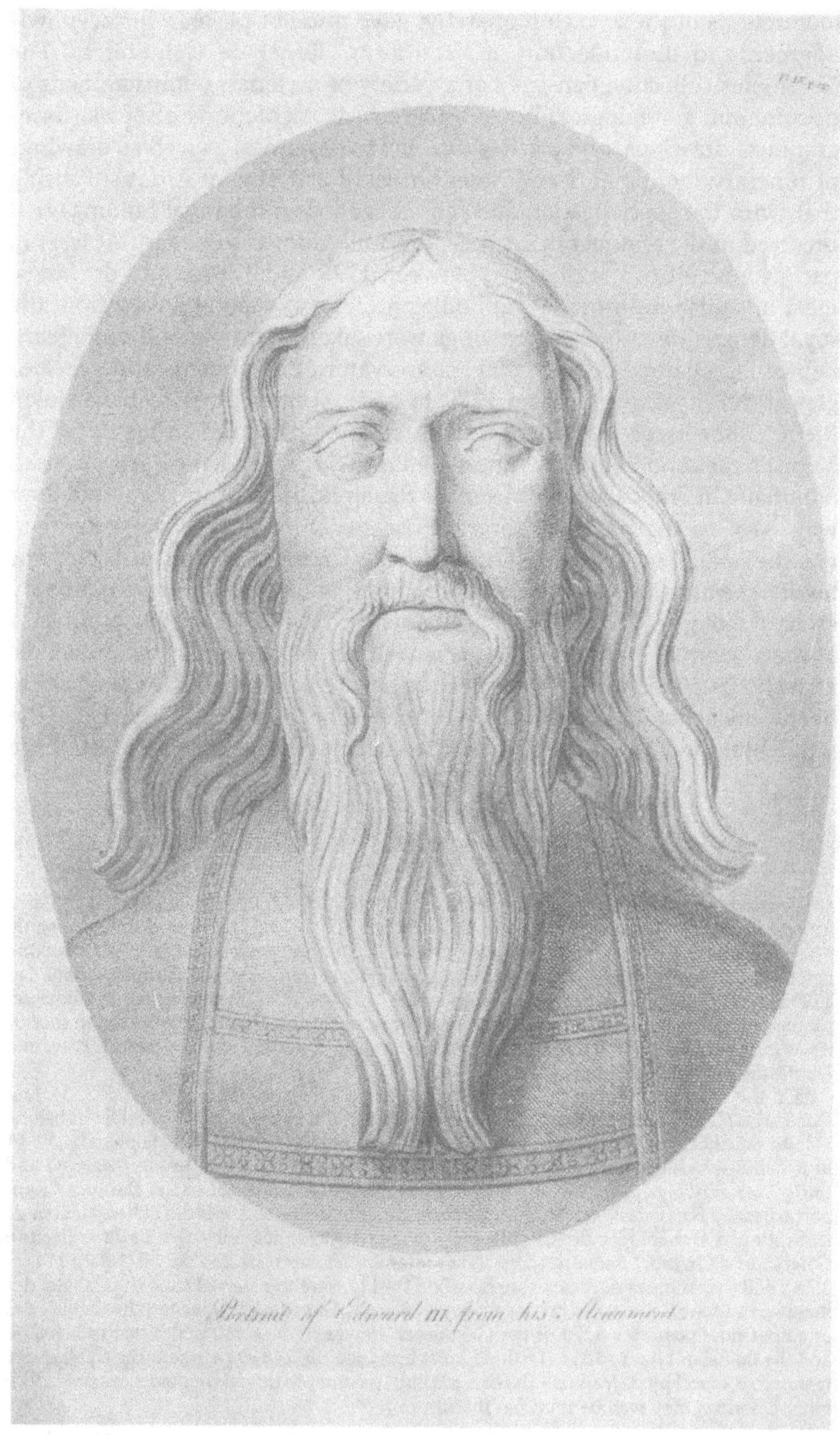

PLATE 1. Portrait and Tomb of Edward III. Gough, *Sepulchral Monuments*, 1: pls. LIV-LV, facing 137 and 139. (Photographic Credit: Elizabeth A. R. Brown; Avery Architectural and Fine Arts Library, Columbia University)

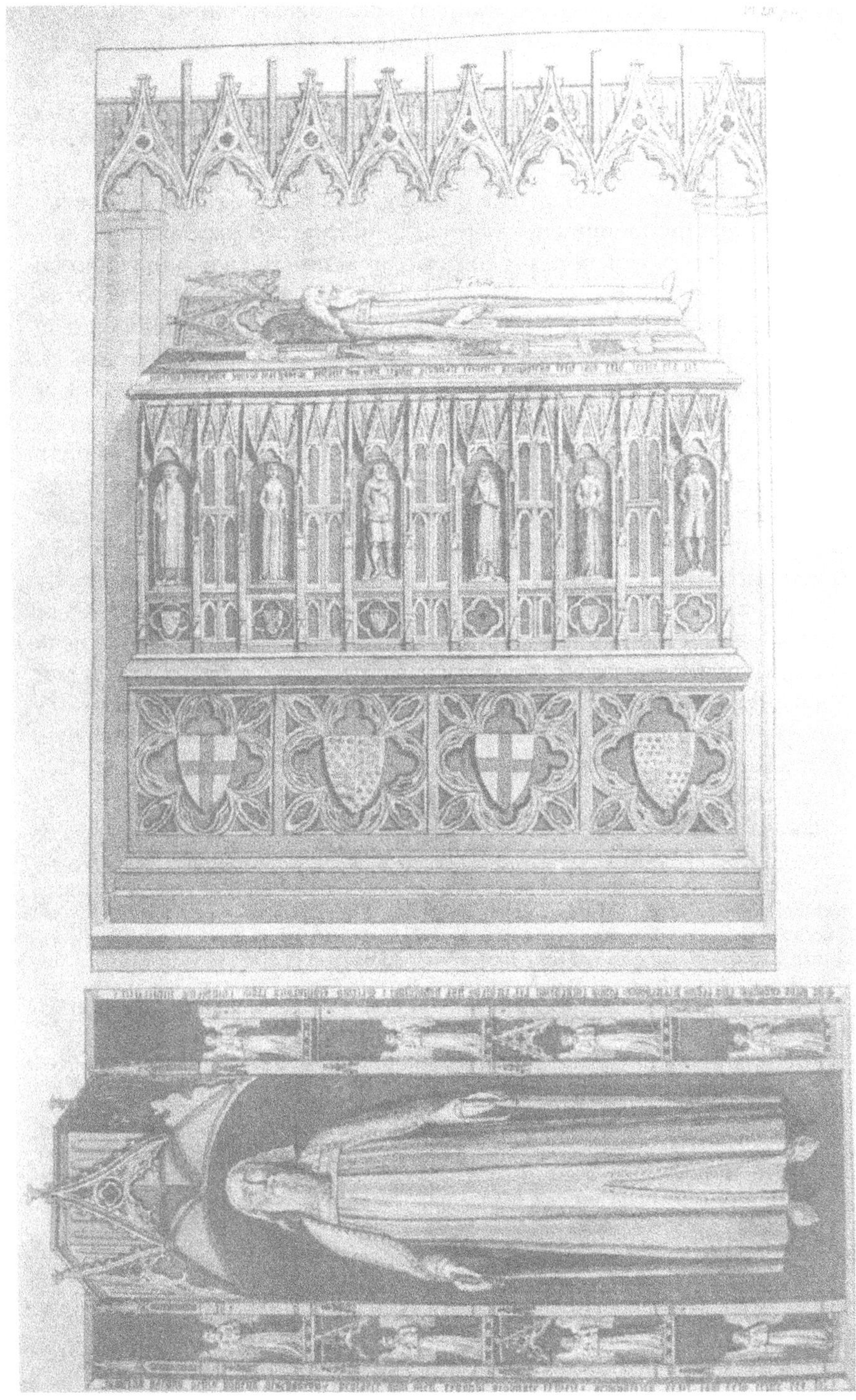

PLATE 1. *(Continued)*

of Montfaucon and, directly or indirectly, Gaignières (plate 1).[7] Before his death in 1809, Gough bequeathed the Gaignières drawings to the Bodleian.[8]

There is no evidence that the drawings removed from the royal library had been much used before their disappearance. Montfaucon, for example, relied on another series in the Gaignières collection for his representations of royalty and nobility. The drawings that Gough acquired were not missed while the monuments that had been recorded for Gaignières survived. However, because of the confusion that resulted when the tombs of the French royal lines were removed from their settings at Saint-Denis during the Revolution, the Gaignières drawings of the memorials would, in the nineteenth century, come to be considered an essential resource for remedying the damage caused in the 1790s, even if they were not as indispensable as the Baron de Guilhermy and Viollet-le-Duc believed. Alexandre Lenoir (1769–1839), more diligent and ingenious than is often acknowledged, used readily available sources to identify correctly most of the monuments that came into his hands. But after the demise of his Musée des monumens français the monuments passed to others who, despite their criticisms of Lenoir, were less clever than he. Their confusion finally resulted in the rediscovery of the Gaignières drawings in Oxford. Once found, the collection's importance as a record of monuments that had been damaged or disappeared was quickly recognized. In the 1840s, 1850s, and 1860s, through reproductions secured for France, the Oxford drawings served practical ends in the hands of those who were determined to revive, in the service of their country, the traces of France's glorious past. Nowhere did they prove more useful than at Saint-Denis.

---

[7] Richard Gough, *Sepulchral Monuments in Great Britain . . .* , 3 vols. (London: Nichols, 1786–99); on Gough, see the study by Thompson Cooper in *Dictionary of National Biography* and the memoir in John Nichols, *Literary Anecdotes of the Eighteenth Century . . .* , 9 vols. (London: Nichols and Bentley, 1812–15), 6: 262–343, especially 329–31. Like Gaignières, Gough had drawn for him not only funerary monuments, but also portraits based on the effigies. For Gough's assessment of Montfaucon, see *Sepulchral Monuments,* 1, 8. A catalogue of a portion of the Gaignières drawings which Gough acquired, probably made for him in the late eighteenth century, is preserved in Bodl., LP 501/131.

[8] William Dunn Macray, *Annals of the Bodleian Library, Oxford. With a Notice of the Earlier Library of the University,* 2nd ed. (Oxford: Clarendon Press, 1890), 285–89, and John Nichols, *Illustrations of the Literary History of the Eighteenth Century. . . ,* 8 vols. (London: Nichols and Bentley et al., 1817–58), 5: 552–53, 556–61, nos. 66–67, 75–78, 81, 84. The sections of Gough's will relevant to the bequest to the Bodleian are published in Bulkeley Bandinel and P. Bliss, *A Catalogue of the Books, Relating to British Topography, and Saxon and Northern Literature, Bequeathed to the Bodleian Library in the Year MDCCXCIX. By Richard Gough, Esq., F.S.A.* (Oxford: Clarendon Press, 1814), 3–4.

I. THE REVOLUTION AND THE ROYAL TOMBS OF FRANCE

By insuring their preservation, the passage of the drawings of the Gaignières collection to England might have been a blessing. During the Revolution, damage and destruction were visited on documents and images considered royal and feudal, and collections similar to that of Gaignières did not emerge unscathed.[9] As to the royal funerary monuments which had been drawn for Gaignières, the revolutionaries were for a time hesitant. In 1791 the Commission des monuments planned to have all such memorials deposited at Saint-Denis,[10] but the progress of the Revolution altered these designs. In 1792 the metal tombs of Saint-Denis were removed for melting. During August 1793 the other memorials which had sheltered the royal bodies were defaced and most of them taken from the church.[11] Alexandre Lenoir could not save the metal tombs or the

---

[9] For the destruction of some 2000 volumes and boxes of genealogical material of the Clairambault collection during the Revolution, see Delisle, *Cabinet des manuscrits,* 2: 24–25. See also Gustave Gautherot, *Le vandalisme Jacobin. Destructions administratives d'archives, d'objets d'art, de monuments religieux . . . ,* 2nd ed. (Paris and Lille: A. Fattin-Lefort, Gabriel Beauchesne, 1914); Ernst Steinmann, "Der Zerstörung der Königsdenkmaler in Paris," *Monatshefte für Kunstwissenschaft* 10 (1917): 337–80; and *Alexandre Lenoir, son journal et le Musée des monuments français,* ed. Louis-Charles-Jean Courajod, 3 vols. (Paris: Honoré Champion, 1878-87), 1: 18–20, 42 (Lenoir's journal for 1792–93).

[10] *Procès-verbaux de la Commission des monuments,* ed. Louis Tuetey, *Nouvelles archives de l'art français;* 3rd ser., 17–18 (1901–02) [*Revue de l'art français ancien et moderne* 18–19 (1902–03)], 17: 29–31 (29 March 1791), 31–33 (17 April 1791), and 40 (5 July 1791).

[11] See the diary of Ferdinand-Albert Gautier, organist of Saint-Denis, in BN, fr. 11681, especially p. 98; the diary is published in part in *Le Cabinet historique* 20, part 1 (1874): 280–303 and 21, part 1 (1875): 36–53, 118–34; see particularly 20, part 1 (1874): 294–95; on the abortive efforts of Lenoir to save the metal monument created for Abbot Suger in 1654, see Alexandre Lenoir, *Musée des monumens français . . . ,* 5 vols. (Paris: Guilleminet, 1800–06), 1: 239–40. See also Max Billard, *Les tombeaux des rois sous la Terreur* (Paris: Perrin, 1907), 35; Roch-François-Ferdinand-Marie-Nolasque (hereafter Ferdinand), Baron de Guilhermy, *Monographie de l'abbaye royale de Saint-Denis* (Paris: Victor Didron, 1848), 84–86; "Collection Guilhermy, Notes historiques et descriptives sur l'Abbaye et Basilique de St. Denis," 2 vols., BN, n.a.f. 6121–6122 (hereafter Guilhermy, BN, n.a.f. 6121 or 6122), particularly n.a.f. 6121, fol. 131; n.a.f. 6122, fol. 185, and the report of Guilhermy of 21 May 1847 in ADP, SSDB, Dossier de l'Administration 1841–1876 (hereafter ADP, SSDB, Dossier 1841–76), fol. 140; AN, F^{21} 1451, Liasse "Eglise St Denis," François Debret, "Eglise Royale de St. Denis 1833. Notes historiques sur la fondation de l'Eglise Royale de St. Denis, Sa dévastation et sa Restauration" (dated 20 December 1832, Paris) (hereafter AN, F^{21} 1451, Debret), 4–5. L.-V. Flamand-Grétry provides a useful survey of events at Saint-Denis between 1793 and 1840 in his *Description complète de la ville de Saint-Denis, depuis son origine jusqu'à nos jours . . .* (Paris and Saint-Denis: Arthus Bertrand and Chichereau, 1840), 107–90. For the defacing of the tombs and the exhumation of the royal bodies, see my article, "Burying and Unburying the Kings of France," in *Persons in Groups. Social Behavior as Identity Formation in Medieval and Renaissance Europe. Papers of the Sixteenth Annual Conference of the Center for Medieval and Early Renaissance Studies,* ed. Richard C. Trexler (Medieval and Renaissance Texts and Studies, 36; Binghamton: Medieval and Renaissance Texts and Studies, 1985), 241–66.

treasury of Saint-Denis. Between late November 1793 and the spring of 1796, however, he succeeded in having transported to the Musée des monumens français, which he established at the Petits-Augustins, the memorial created for Dagobert in the 1240s, the sixteen royal tombs erected in the crossing in the 1260s, and the monuments of later kings installed at Saint-Denis.[12] At Lenoir's museum, these gisants and many effigies from other churches were eventually displayed in a number of impressive rooms, chronologically and historically arranged (plate 2). The huge and impressive memorial to Dagobert was placed in Lenoir's park, the "Elysée," adjoining his museum.[13]

For his museum and catalogues, Lenoir had to identify the monuments he had gathered from Saint-Denis and other sites. The sixteen stylized gisants of Saint-Denis that were created during Saint Louis's reign posed particular problems. They were barely individualized, and, abruptly dislodged from the crossing of Saint-Denis, they had been separated from their mountings and inscriptions. Nonetheless, Lenoir's identifications of these monuments and others, recorded in the catalogue of his museum, were, with few exceptions, remarkably accurate (plate 3).

Lenoir used a number of sources to identify the monuments he collected. He relied particularly on Montfaucon's volumes,[14] many of whose repre-

---

[12] AN, F^{21} 1451, Debret, 5. Cf. Alain Erlande-Brandenburg, *Le roi est mort. Etude sur les funérailles, les sépultures et les tombeaux des rois de France jusqu'à la fin du XIIIe siècle* (Bibliothèque de la Société française d'archéologie, 7; Geneva: Droz, 1975), 149–54, 158–61. Erlande-Brandenburg states that the effigies of Eudes and of Hugues Capet disappeared in 1793, and he suggests that they may have been used to create the Montagne at Saint-Denis, prominently featuring three gisants, which was sketched by or for Lenoir: ibid., 158, nos. 71–72, n. 1; see also Brown, "Burying and Unburying," 253–54, fig. 6, and 264, n. 16; and Lenoir's report of 20 December 1793, in *Inventaire général des richesses d'art de la France. Archives du Musée des monuments français,* 3 vols. (Paris: Plon, 1883–87), 1: 16, no. XVII. According to Billard, it was the gisants of Carloman (II?) and of Clovis II that in October 1794 were used for the Montagne. He, like Erlande-Brandenburg, states (without citing any source) that the tombs of Eudes and Hugues Capet were destroyed at the time of the Revolution: Billard, *Tombeaux,* 36–37, who attributes the sketch of the Montagne to Percier. For the arrival of the first monuments from Saint-Denis at Lenoir's museum, see Courajod, 1: 21, no. 166; for 1793 see *Inventaire général des richesses,* 1: 14–15, no. XVII and cf. 29–30; see ibid. 2: 78, no. LXII; for 1794, ibid. 2: 218–19, no. CLXI; for the final list sent to the temporary Commission des arts on 8 February 1795, ibid. 2: 231–32, no. CLXXVI. On the thirteenth-century monuments at Saint-Denis, see Georgia Sommers Wright, "A Royal Tomb Program in the Reign of St. Louis," *Art Bulletin* 56 (1974): 224–43, especially 231, 235–36; and Maryse Bideault, "Le tombeau de Dagobert dans l'abbaye royale de Saint-Denis," *Revue de l'Art* 18 (1972): 27–33.

[13] See Alain Erlande-Brandenburg, "Alexandre Lenoir et le Musée des Monuments français," in *Le "Gothique" retrouvé avant Viollet-le-Duc* (Paris: Caisse nationale des monuments historiques, 1979), 75–84; and Dominique Poulot, "Alexandre Lenoir et les Musées des Monuments français," in Pierre Nora et al., *Les lieux de mémoire, II, La Nation,* 3 vols. (Paris: Gallimard, 1986), 2: 496–531. For depictions of the museum, see Jean-Baptiste-Bonaventure de Roquefort and Vauzelle, *Vues pittoresques et perspectives des salles du Musée des monuments françois . . .* (Paris: P. Didot aîné, 1816), and J.-E. Biet and Jean-Pierre Brès, *Souvenirs du Musée des monuments français. Collection de 40 dessins perspectifs* (Paris: Normand fils, 1821); some of Biet's drawings are reproduced in Courajod, vol. 2; see also Georges Huard, "La salle du XIIIe siècle du Musée des Monuments français à l'Ecole des Beaux-Arts," *Revue de l'Art,* 29e année, 47 (1925): 118.

[14] See Lenoir, *Musée,* 1: 168, and 2: cxi, cxviii.

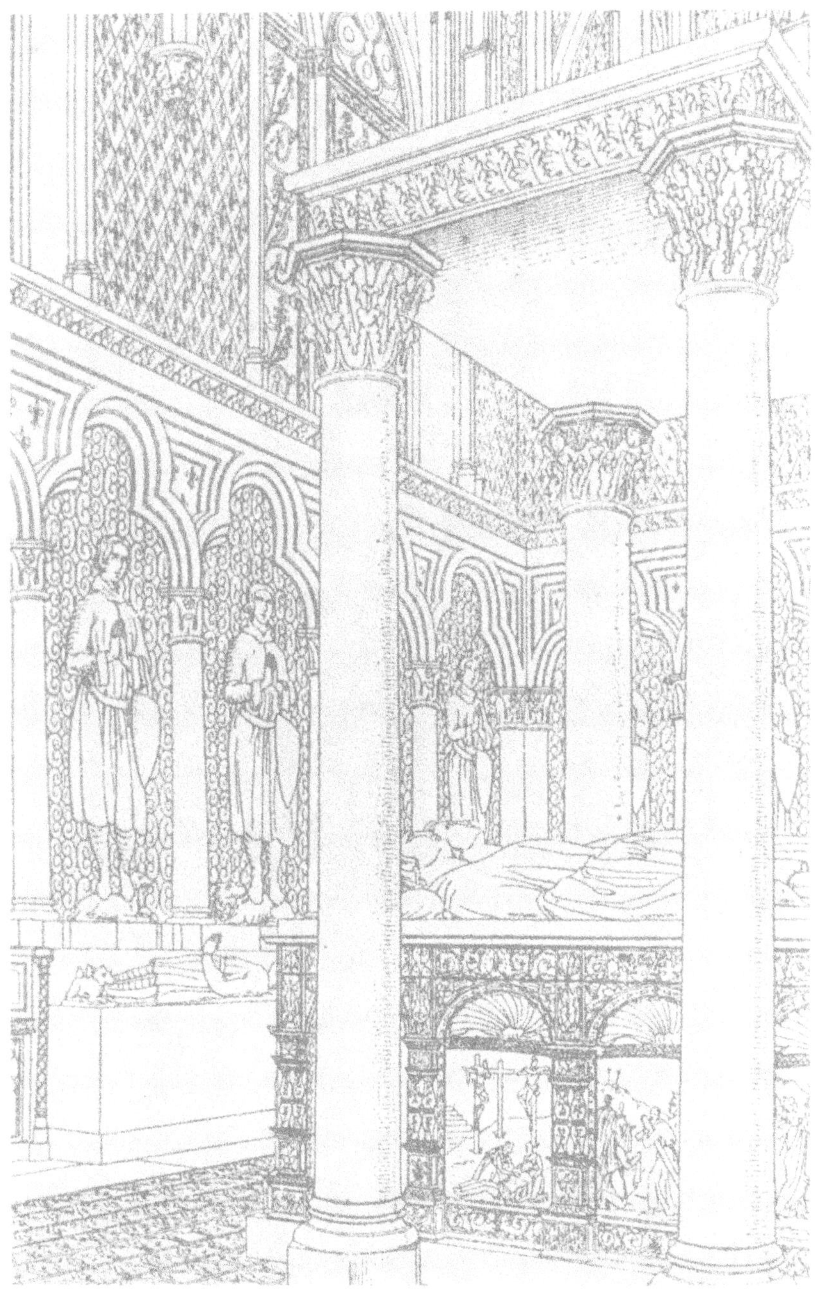

PLATE 2. Musée des monumens français. Salle du XIVe siècle. After Biet and Brès, *Souvenirs du Musée des monuments français*, pl. XVIII, IIe, "Vue de la Salle du XIVe. siècle." In Courajod, 2: facing 38. (Photographic Credit: Elizabeth A. R. Brown; Avery Architectural and Fine Arts Library, Columbia University)

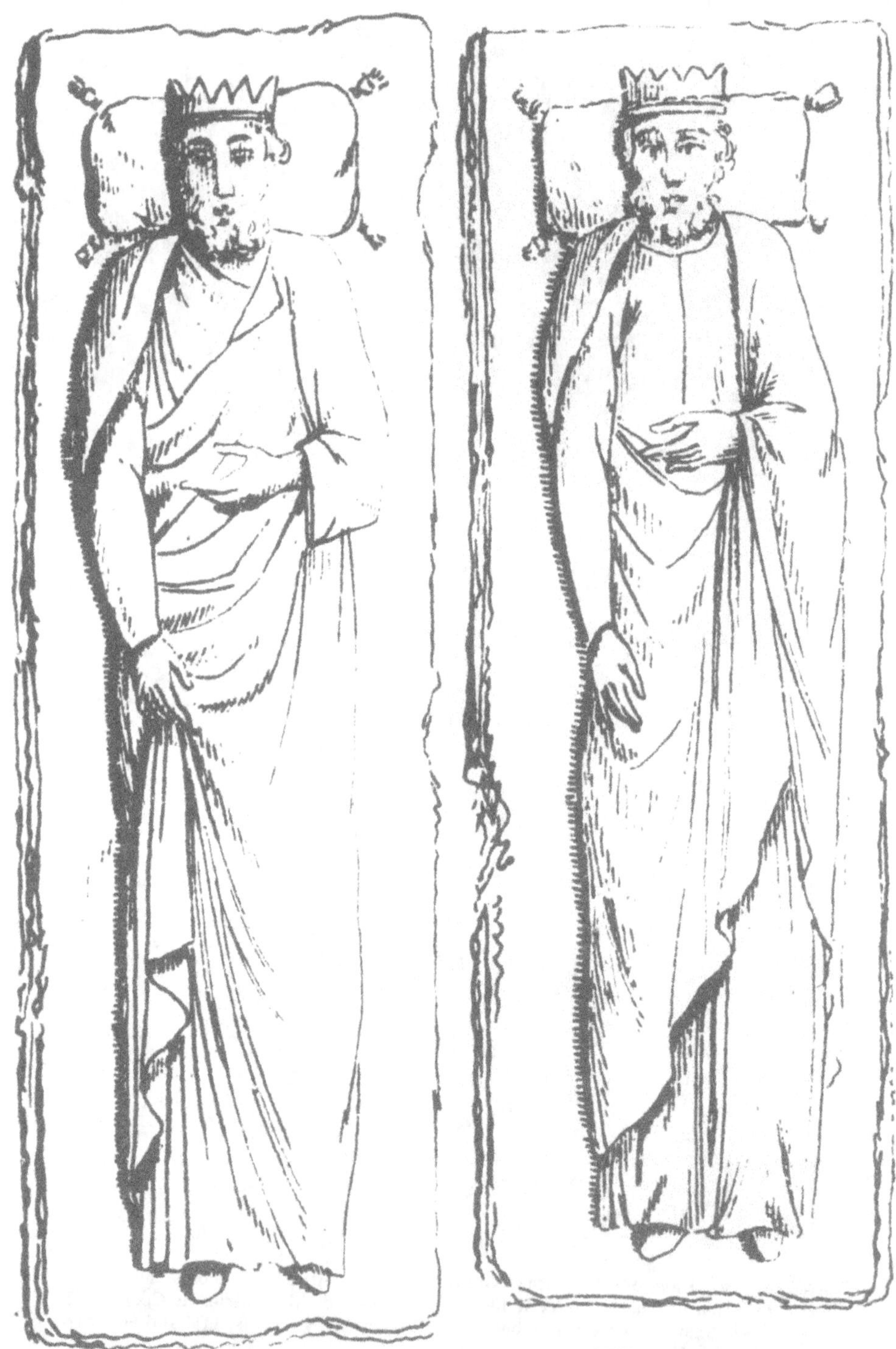

PLATE 3. Effigies of Eudes and Hugues Capet (reversed in plate). Lenoir, *Musée,* 1: pl. 27, nos. 15 and 16, facing p. 186. (Photographic Credit: Avery Architectural and Fine Arts Library, Columbia University)

sentations of individual royalty were based on the series of drawings in the Gaignières collection which, modeled on the gisants, presented those whom they portrayed in life-like poses (plate 4).[15] Although Montfaucon's engravings were later criticized as inaccurate,[16] they in fact provide faithful images of the tombs, reproducing as they do the gestures and garb of the effigies (plate 5). There is no evidence that Lenoir utilized the original Gaignières drawings rather than the engravings in Montfaucon's volumes, which were perfectly serviceable for his purposes. So too were the minuscule but faithful depictions of the tombs of the abbey's crossing (plate 6) which Félibien had published in his history of Saint-Denis in 1706.[17]

There is only one possible error in Lenoir's identifications of the monuments created in the thirteenth century. In an early, unpolished version of his catalogue, published in 1796–97, Lenoir identified the effigy of Carloman I, son of Pepin (paired with that of Hermentrude, wife of Charles the Bald) as Charles the Bald's—whose metal tomb had in fact been melted in 1792. In his catalogue of 1800, having correctly stated that the gisant was Carloman's, Lenoir confusingly reproduced a sentence from the earlier version which asserted that Louis IX had had Charles the Bald's original tomb, "détruit par vétusté," replaced by this memorial. Lenoir later alternated between identifying the male effigy as Carloman's and presenting it as Charles the Bald's.[18]

Lenoir's identifications of effigies from other churches were less reliable, as the Baron de Guilhermy later pointed out. Guilhermy criticized Lenoir for labeling an effigy he himself associated with Catherine of Courtenay as

---

[15] Montfaucon's engravings of the tomb figures created in the 1260s appear in 1: pl. XIII, no. 2, facing 164 (Clovis II); pl. XIX, nos. 1–5, facing 272 (Charles Martel, Pepin, Berthe, Carloman I, and Hermentrude, wrongly identified as Gerberge, wife of Carloman); pl. XXIX, nos. 1, 2, 4, facing 306 (Clovis III, Carloman II, and Eudes); pl. XXXIII, nos. 1, 2, 4, facing 370 (Hugues Capet, Robert, and Constance of Arles); pl. XXXIV, no. 1, following 370 (Henri I); 2: pl. X, nos. 1–2, facing 48 (Louis VI, and Philip his son); pl. XII, no. 4, preceding 71 (Constance of Castile, whose tomb Montfaucon mistakenly says was located with that of her husband Louis VII at Barbeaux; cf. Aubin-Louis Millin de Grandmaison, *Antiquités nationales*, 5 vols. [Paris: Drouhin, 1790–98], 2: art. XIII [Abbaye de Barbeau], 13). For the Gaignières drawings on which Montfaucon's engravings were based, see Bouchot, *Inventaire général des richesses*, 1: 5–161, the series "Costumes," BN, RE, Oa 9-Ob 10a.

[16] ADP, SSDB, Dossier 1841–76, fol. 34 (François Debret, 14 January 1842); Guilhermy, BN, n.a.f. 6122, fol. 191; and ADP, SSDB, Dossier 1841–76, fol. 143v.

[17] Michel Félibien, *Histoire de l'abbaye royale de Saint-Denys en France* (Paris: Frederic Leonard, 1706; reprint, with introduction by Hervé Pinoteau, Paris: Editions du Palais Royal, 1973), pl. facing 550.

[18] See Lenoir, *Musée*, 1: pl. 26, facing 184; pl. 27, facing 186; and pl. 28, facing 168; for Carloman/Charles the Bald and Hermentrude, ibid. 1: 185, no. 13; and 8: 173, no. 13; see also, for Carloman, *Inventaire général des richesses*, 1: 406, no. CCCCXXVI (2 April 1811), and AN, F^{17A} 1280A, Dossier 7 of Liasse "3e Division, Bureau des Beaux-Arts, Musée des monuments français 1811" (8 August 1811); for Charles the Bald, see Alexandre Lenoir, *Musée royal des monumens français, ou, Mémorial de l'histoire de France et de ses monumens* (Paris: Chez l'auteur, 1815), 63, no. 15; see also *Inventaire général des richesses*, 3: 157, nos. 18–19, no. CCCCLXXIX; 242, nos. 18–19, no. XD; 287, no. 13, no. DIX (documents relating to the dispersal of the monuments of the Petits-Augustins, in which Lenoir identified the male gisant as Charles the Bald's); see also, however, Courajod, 1: 181, no. 13 (a similar document from the period of the dissolution of the museum, where the gisant is said to be Carloman's).

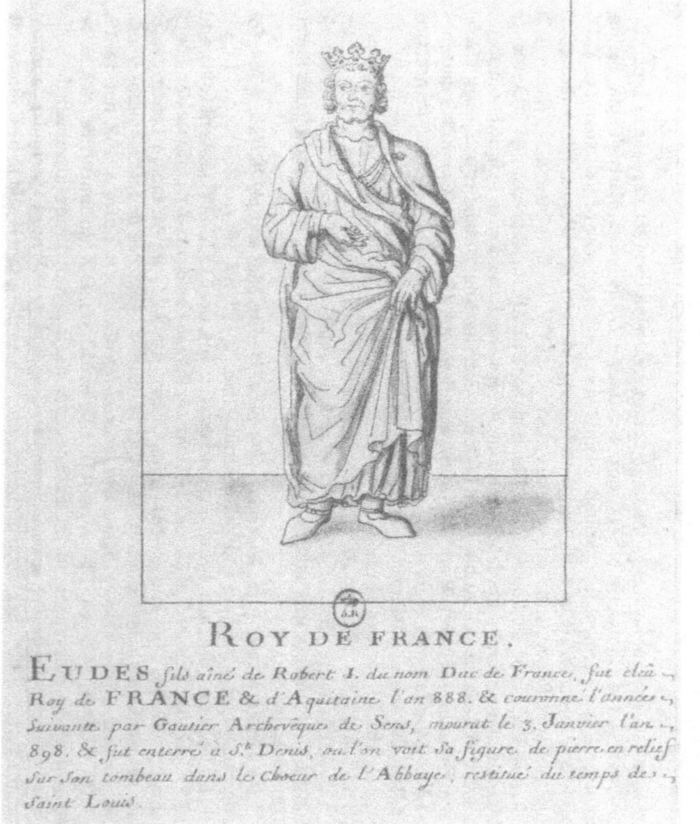

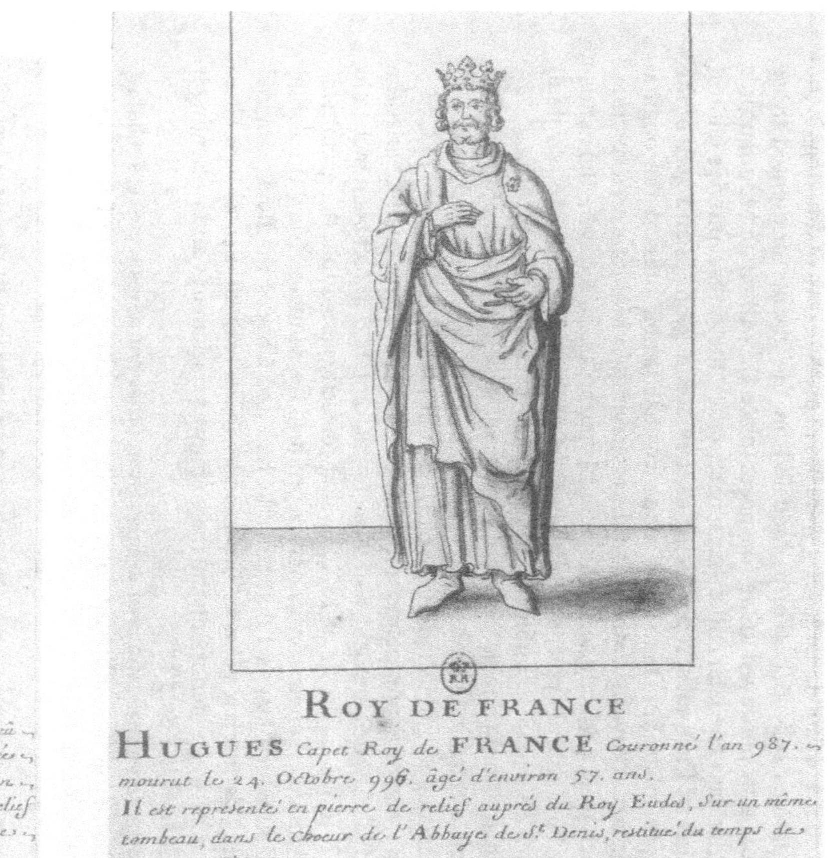

PLATE 4. Gaignières Drawings of a) Eudes and b) Hugues Capet. Paris, Bibliothèque nationale, Réserve des estampes, Oa 9, fols. 19, 21 (C 55407 and 63717). (Photographic Credit: Paris, Bibliothèque nationale)

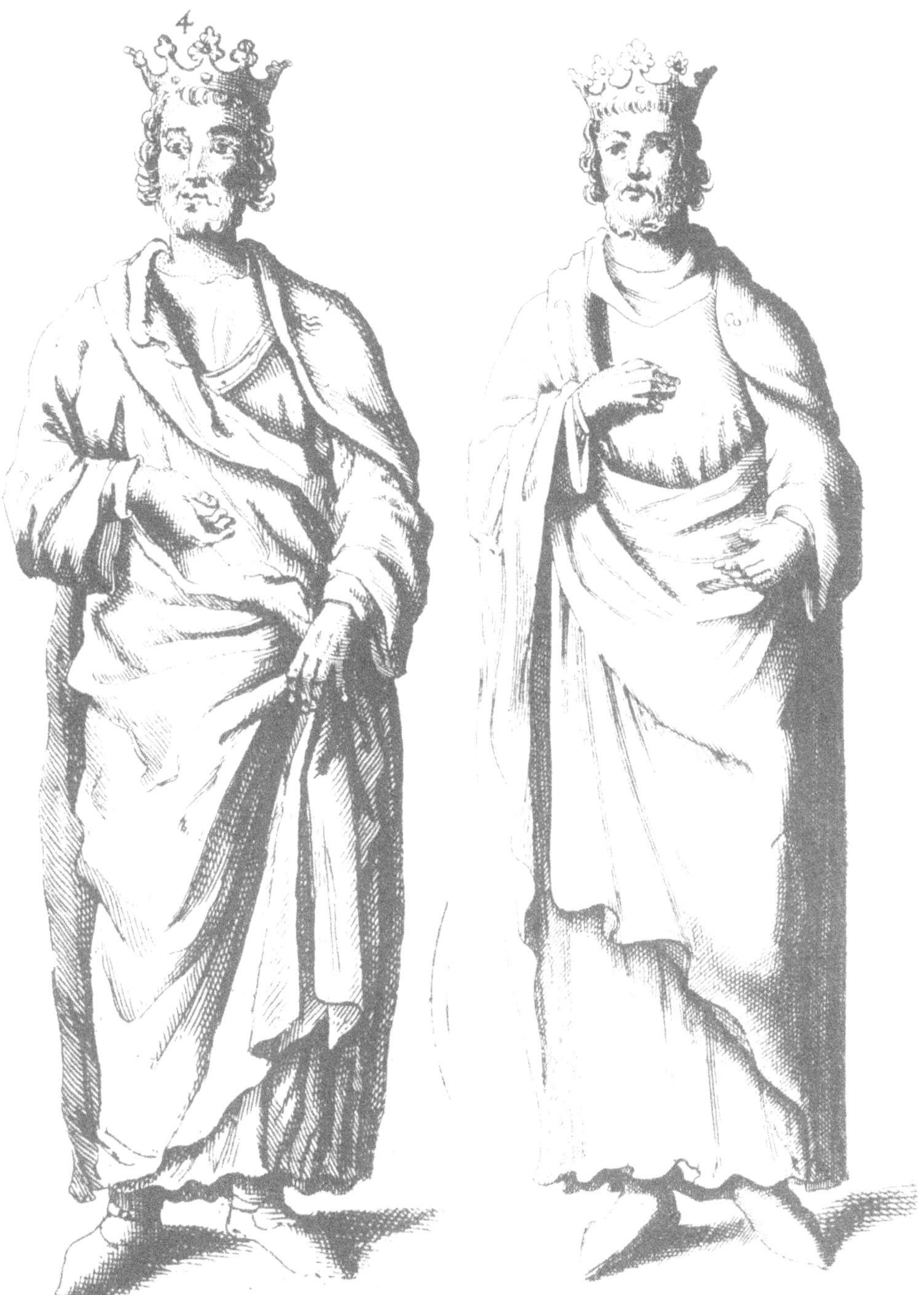

PLATE 5. Eudes and Hugues Capet. Montfaucon, *Monumens,* 1: pl. XXIX, no. 4, facing 306, and pl. XXXIII, no. 1, facing 370. (Photographic Credit: Avery Architectural and Fine Arts Library, Columbia University)

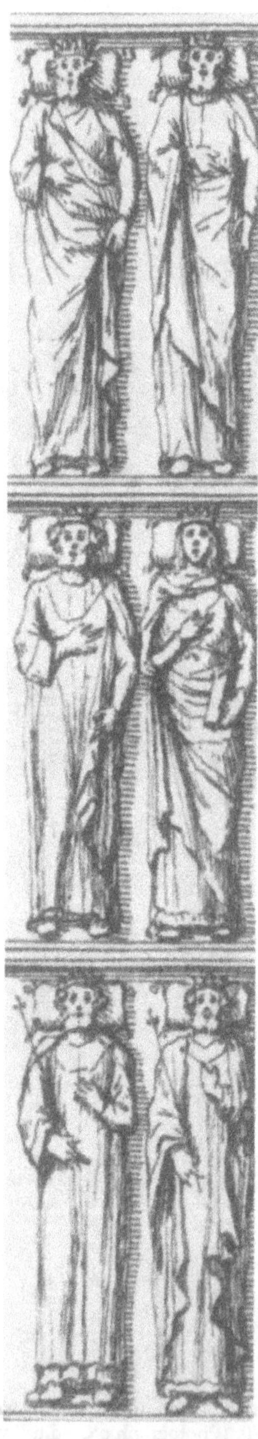

PLATE 6. Three Pairs of Tombs in the Crossing of Saint-Denis (from top to bottom and left to right: Eudes and Hugues Capet; Robert and Constance; Henri I and Louis VI). Félibien, *Histoire*, taken from plate facing p. 500. (Photographic Credit: Elizabeth A. R. Brown; Avery Architectural and Fine Arts Library, Columbia University)

that of Blanche of Castile, for identifying the effigy of Charles of Valois as that of Robert of Clermont, *sieur* of Bourbon, and for attaching the name of Pierre of Alençon to a monument bearing armorial devices that were not his. He went so far as to charge that "Mr. Lenoir semble du reste avoir commis sciemment [ces trois erreurs capitales]," errors which had been perpetuated through copies of the monuments installed at Versailles. Waxing more eloquent, he later said that "on eut le tort impardonable de chercher à tromper le public, en décorant de noms illustres des statues qui ne représentaient que des personnages obscurs."[19]

As will be seen, Guilhermy's accusations had some foundation in truth as regards the effigy of Charles of Valois. In the case of the gisant of the "princesse inconnue" from Maubuisson (Catherine of Courtenay/Blanche of Castile), however, the identification is still not secure,[20] and even Guilhermy himself did not pretend that he could precisely identify the tomb Lenoir assigned to Pierre of Alençon. The latter effigy came from the church of the Cordeliers in Paris, where in 1580 a fire had destroyed many monuments and inscriptions.[21] In 1790 Lenoir believed—as others previously had done—that the tomb sheltered the heart of Philip V.[22] By 1794 he had decided (quite wrongly) that it was the gisant of Pierre of Alençon, son of Saint Louis, whose body was buried at the Cordeliers.[23] On what

---

[19] Guilhermy, BN, n.a.f. 6121, fol. 160v, and n.a.f. 6122, fol. 189.

[20] See Françoise Baron, "La gisante en pierre de Tournai de la Cathédrale de Saint-Denis," *Bulletin monumental* 128 (1970): 211–28, who suggests that it is that of Mahaut of Artois; cf. Alain Erlande-Brandenburg, "Le Moyen Age," in Alain Erlande-Brandenburg, Jean-Pierre Babelon, Françoise Jenn, and Jean-Marie Jenn, *Le roi, la sculpture et la mort. Gisants et tombeaux de la Basilique de Saint-Denis* (Saint-Denis: Archives départementales de la Seine-Saint-Denis, Bulletin no. 3, June 1975), 15–16, no. 24.

[21] This gisant (and those of Charles of Etampes and of Blanche, daughter of Louis IX, which Lenoir also claimed) were among the few effigies to survive the fire: Gilles Corrozet, *Les Antiqvitez Croniqves et Singvlaritez de Paris . . .* , ed. Nicolas Bonfons, 2 vols. (Paris: Nicolas Bonfons, 1586–88), 1: fols. 86v, 198v–99; Jacques Du Breul, *Le theatre des antiqvitez de Paris* (Paris: P. Chevalier, 1612), 537. According to Du Breul, only five funerary monuments were preserved "entiers" in 1612: that of Blanche of France, the paired monument of an unidentified count and countess, two non-royal effigies, and "le tombeau d'un prince armé, son escu semé de fleurs de lys à quatre lambeaux": Du Breul, 520–23.

[22] See Lenoir's report of 15 December 1790, where he described the gisant's arms as "parsemés de fleurs de lis sans nombre": *Inventaire général des richesses,* 1: 3, no. III. The drawing of this tomb made for Gaignières (Adhémar, "Tombeaux," no. 611) was not specifically identified; the tomb was simply said to be "dans le coeur des Cordeliers a droite du grand autel": BN, Clairambault 632, fol. 166. Its placement in Gaignières's collection with drawings and documents related to Philip of Poitiers (later Philip V) indicates, however, that Gaignières—or perhaps Clairambault, who gained possession of this part of the Gaignières collection—assigned it to Philip V. The arms of Philip as count of Poitiers which are depicted immediately preceding the drawing of the gisant show, however, a label of five, rather than four, points: BN, Clairambault 632, fol. 165v. Since Philip died as king of France, any memorial erected for him at the Cordeliers would surely have shown him as king, not as count of Poitiers. For the inscription on the heart tomb of Philip V at the Cordeliers, see Corrozet, *Antiqvitez,* 1: fol. 83v. In the 1770s the tomb was identified at the church as that of Charles of Etampes (d. 1336), son of Louis of Evreux: see Appendix II.

[23] Anselme de Sainte-Marie, *Histoire genealogique et chronologique de la maison royale de France,* 3rd ed., ed. les P. Ange and Simplicien, 9 vols. (Paris: Compagnie des Libraires, 1726–33), 1: 86. No reference to any tomb or inscription connected with Pierre of Alençon is found in Corrozet or Du Breul. In November 1793 Lenoir received various monuments from the Cordeliers, among which he listed two warriors' effigies, identified as sons of Saint Louis.

basis he did so is unclear. The arms shown on the effigy's buckler in Lenoir's catalogue (plate 7) (*semé de France à la bordure de gueules, au lambel de trois pendants*) were not Pierre's (which were *semé de France à la bordure de gueules*). Nor indeed are they those that actually adorned the gisant (plate 8).[24] As Guilhermy later noted, and as Lenoir could have discovered, the arms (*semé de France, au lambel de quatre pendants*) were those of the house of Artois. Not until 1879, however, did Jules-Marie Richard identify the effigy as that of Robert l'Enfant, son of Otto of Burgundy and Mahaut of Artois, who was also buried at the Cordeliers.[25]

If the mistakes Lenoir made in identifying these two gisants are understandable, the same cannot be said of his erroneous designation of the tomb of Charles of Valois as that of Robert of Clermont, founder of the Bourbon line. According to Lenoir, the tomb, originally at the church of the Jacobins of the rue Saint-Jacques in Paris, was adorned with Robert's epitaphs, of which one, behind the head, was "brisée"; in an early catalogue he stated that "des malveillans ont mutilé cette statue."[26] By consulting Montfaucon's engraving of Robert's effigy (plate 9) and Millin's detailed description of it,[27] Lenoir could readily have determined that the gisant was not Robert's—particularly since the effigy he actually pos-

---

In his proposed catalogue, submitted in 1794, he designated the gisants as Pierre of Alençon and (in this case correctly) Charles of Etampes: *Inventaire général des richesses*, 2: 94, no. LXXXII; 103–4, no. LXXXV; and 177, no. CXLI. These identifications were given to the gisants while they were in his museum: Alexandre Lenoir, *Description historique et chronologique des monuments de sculpture, réunis au Musée des Monumens français . . .*, 3rd ed. (Paris: Au Musée, An V de la République [1796–97]), 66, no. 25, and 74–75, no. 48; idem, *Musée*, 1: 197 and pl. 31, no. 25, facing p. 196, and 2: 62 and pl. 66, no. 48, facing p. 68; 8: 174–75, nos. 25, 48; idem, *Musée royal* (1815), 66, no. 25, and 70, no. 48; *Inventaire général des richesses*, 3: 158, no. CCCCLXXIX; 166, no. CCCCLXXX; 243, no. XD; 244, no. XDI; 288, no. DIX. Although the effigy of Charles of Etampes was drawn for Gaignières (Adhémar, "Tombeaux," no. 704), no depiction of it appeared in the printed guides to Paris.

[24] The tomb is now at Saint-Denis, in the northern ambulatory: Alain Erlande-Brandenburg, *L'église abbatiale de Saint-Denis*, vol. 2, *Les tombeaux royaux* (Collection. "Les Belles Eglises de Paris"; Bellegarde: SCOP-SADAG, 1976), no. 27 in fig. 7 and p. [14], and in *Le roi, la sculpture et la mort*, 17.

[25] Guilhermy, *Monographie*, 253–55, and the pl. facing 253; Jules-Marie Richard, "Robert l'Enfant aux Cordeliers de Paris," *Mémoires de la Société de l'histoire de Paris et de l'Ile-de-France* 6 (1879), 290–304; idem, *Une petite-nièce de Saint Louis. Mahaut, comtesse d'Artois et de Bourgogne (1302–1329)* . . . (Paris: H. Champion, 1887), 316–17; Françoise Baron, "Un artiste du XIVe siècle: Jean Pépin de Huy. Problèmes d'attribution," *Bulletin de la Société de l'histoire de l'art français* (1960): 89; and Erlande-Brandenburg, in *Le roi, la sculpture et la mort*, 17, no. 27. For the similarities, noted by Richard, between the surviving effigy and that of Robert l'Enfant's uncle, Philip of Artois, lord of Conches (on which the arms of Artois are clearly shown) compare the plate in Guilhermy's book with the depiction of Philip of Artois in Montfaucon, 2: pl. XXXVIII, no. 5, following p. 214 and in Millin, *Antiquités nationales*, 4: art. XXXIX ("Couvent des Jacobins de la rue Saint-Jacques"), pl. 10, no. 5, p. 67; cf. Bouchot, no. 177. The arms of Artois can also be found in Anselme, 1: 381–85. The tomb of Philip of Artois, once at the Jacobins, was apparently destroyed during the Revolution.

[26] Lenoir, *Description historique*, 72, no. 42; idem, *Musée*, 1: 203–5 and pl. 33, no. 29, facing p. 204; 8: 174, no. 19; idem, *Musée royal* (1815), 66, no. 29. The epitaphs published by Lenoir were in all likelihood copied from Corrozet, *Antiqvitez*, 1: fol. 81, or from Millin, *Antiquités nationales*, 4: art. XXXIX, 63–64.

[27] Montfaucon, 2: pl. 27, no. 10, following p. 162 and see also 161–62, and BN, lat. 11913, no. 8; Millin, *Antiquités nationales*, 4: art. XXXIX, 62.

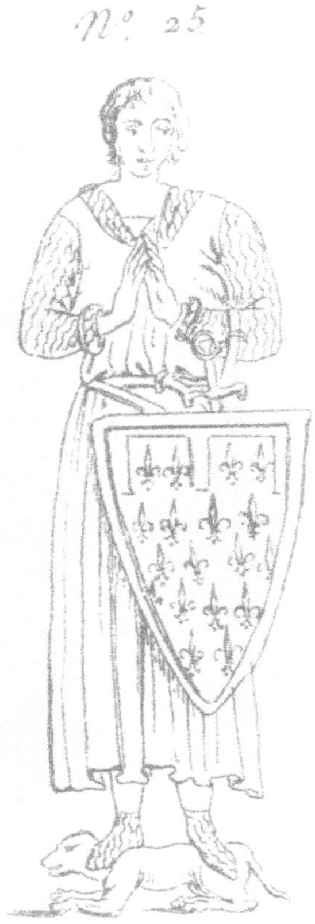

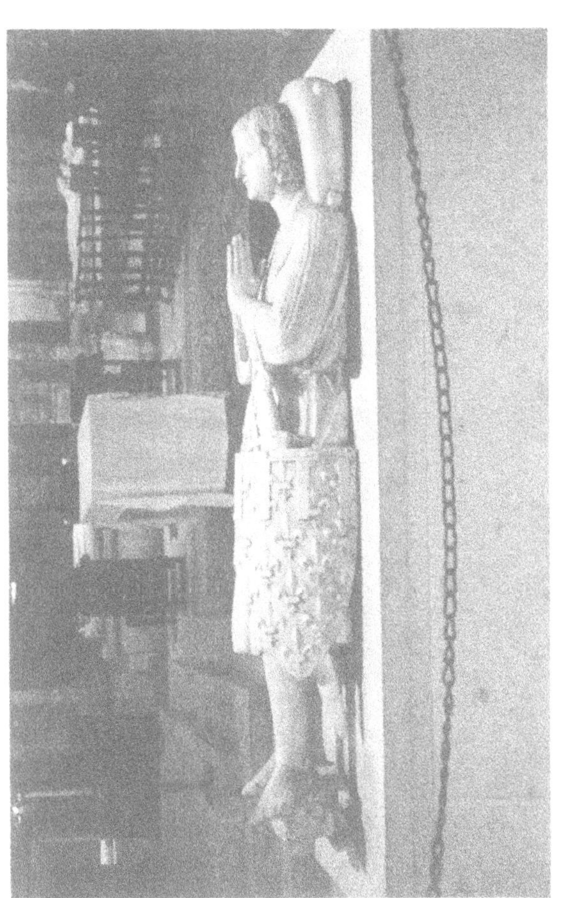

PLATE 7. "Pierre of Alençon" (probably Robert l'Enfant of Artois). Lenoir, *Musée*, 1: pl. 31, no. 25, facing 196. (Photographic Credit: Elizabeth A. R. Brown; Avery Architectural and Fine Arts Library, Columbia University)

PLATE 8. Effigy of Robert l'Enfant of Artois. Cathedral of Saint-Denis (Photographic Credit: Elizabeth A. R. Brown)

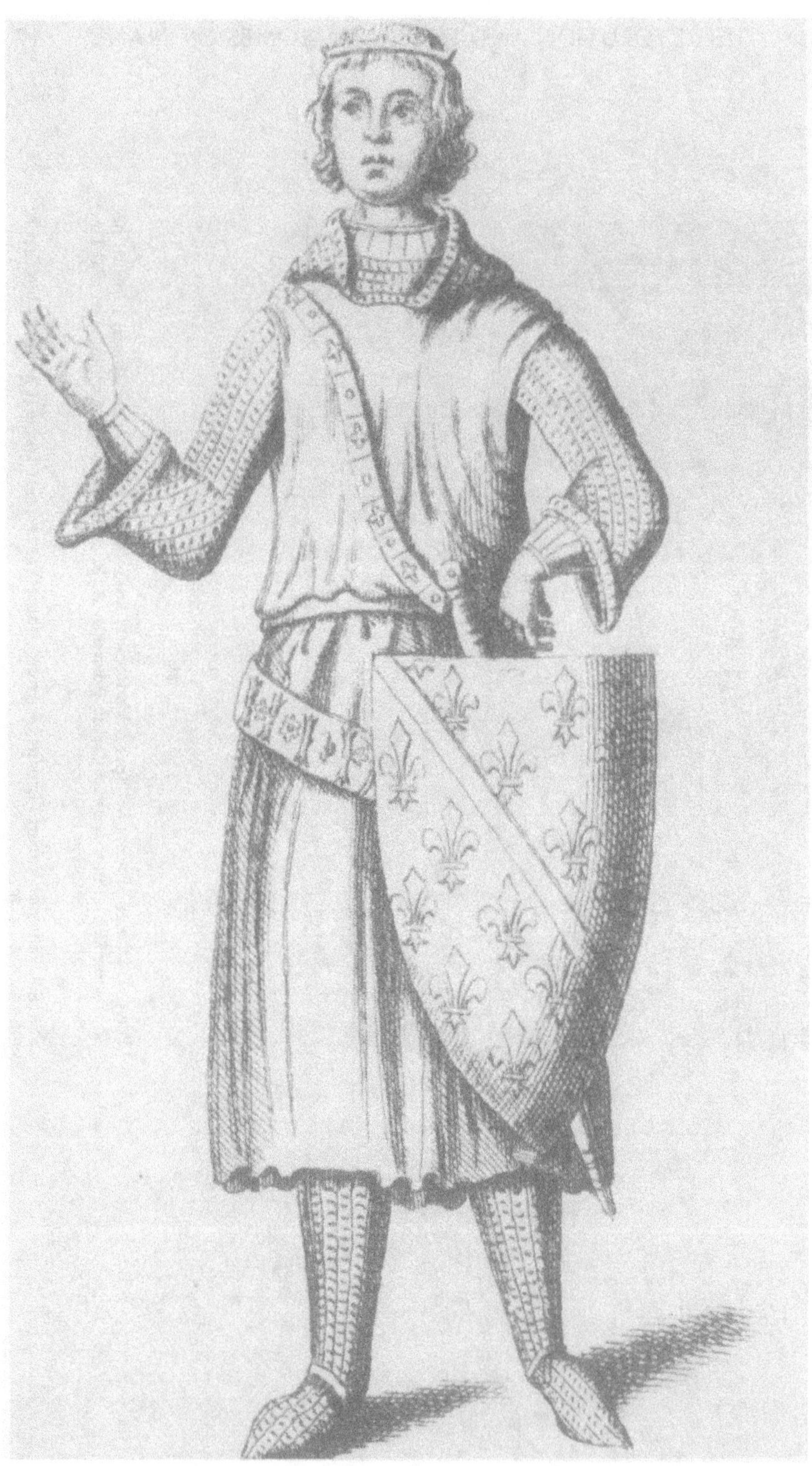

PLATE 9. Robert of Clermont, *sieur* of Bourbon. Montfaucon, *Monumens*, 2: pl. XXVII, no. 10, following 162. (Photographic Credit: Elizabeth A. R. Brown; Avery Architectural and Fine Arts Library, Columbia University)

sessed, that of Charles of Valois, was depicted in Corrozet's and Bonfons's guides to Parisian monuments (plates 10a and 10b).[28] Indeed, Lenoir seems to have known from the beginning that the effigy in his museum was that of Charles of Valois. The projected catalogue of 1794 (which contained no reference to Robert of Clermont) stated that he had received from the Jacobins the tomb of "Charles de France, premier des Valois, fils de Philippe III, mort en 1325."[29] Nonetheless, only once did Lenoir later suggest, in a confused reference in his catalogue of 1815, that he possessed the effigy of Charles of Valois, brother of Philip the Fair.[30] As the first of the Bourbon line, Robert of Clermont had special importance. Thus Lenoir's published catalogue and subsequent lists of monuments in his museum proudly announced that the monument of Charles of Valois was the gisant of Robert of Clermont, "premier des Bourbons." It is perhaps no accident that the image of the gisant published in Lenoir's catalogue of 1801 (plate 11) does not show the arms on the buckler, which would have given the lie to his claims.

Whatever Lenoir's mistakes, the gravest errors in identifying the tombs of Saint-Denis were made later. Following the decree of 24 April 1816 (ordering the restoration of tombs to Saint-Denis) and that of 18 December 1816 (commanding the replacement of Lenoir's museum by the Ecole des Beaux Arts), the Musée des monumens français was closed.[31] Lenoir's museum had been threatened before. After having planned in 1806 to have Lenoir's funerary monuments deposited at Sainte-Geneviève and to transform Saint-Denis into an imperial mausoleum, Napoleon decreed on 24 February 1811 that the tombs in Lenoir's museum should be divided between Saint-Denis and Sainte-Geneviève, which was to receive the remains of notable *savants*. Plans to install the royal memorials in the crypt of Saint-Denis were carefully formulated, but on that occasion Lenoir's

[28] Corrozet, 2: 90, an engraving by Jean Rabel (and see 90v for the standing statue of Charles which was also in the church); this engraving was reproduced in subsequent editions of Corrozet's work and in the guides of Pierre Bonfons, one of which Debret claimed to have consulted (ADP, SSDB, Dossier 1841–1876, fol. 33v); Millin, *Antiquités nationales*, 4: art. XXXIX, pl. 6, no. 4, facing p. 51.

[29] *Inventaire général des richesses*, 2: 94, no. LXXII.

[30] Lenoir, *Description historique*, 72, no. 42; Lenoir, *Musée*, 1: 203–5 and pl. 33, no. 29, facing p. 204; *Inventaire général des richesses*, 3: 159, no. 41, no. CCCCLXXIX; 164, no. 29, no. CCCCLXXXX; 243, no. 41, no. XD; 244, no. 29, no. XDI; 288, no. 29, no. DIX. Hennin indicates that Lenoir exhibited the tomb of Charles of Valois in his museum, but although Lenoir's catalogue of 1815 stated that the effigy of Charles of Valois which he possessed was that of the brother of Philip the Fair, "premier de la branche des Valois," he also said that this Charles, whose tomb was at the church of the Jacobins of the rue Saint-Jacques, died at Crécy on 26 August 1346: Hennin, *Monuments*, 4: 257–58; Lenoir, *Musée royal* (1815), 69, no. 46. Lenoir's earlier catalogues of 1796–97 and 1801 correctly identified the gisant as that of Charles II of Valois, count of Alençon and Perche, "premier de sa branche," who had indeed died at Crécy: Lenoir, *Description historique*, 74, nos. 46 and 54, and *Musée*, 2: 62, no. 46 and pl. 66, no. 46, facing p. 62, and 74, no. 54, and pl. 68, no. 54, facing p. 69.

[31] *Inventaire général des richesses*, 1: 404–11, nos. CCCCXXV–CCCCXXVIII.

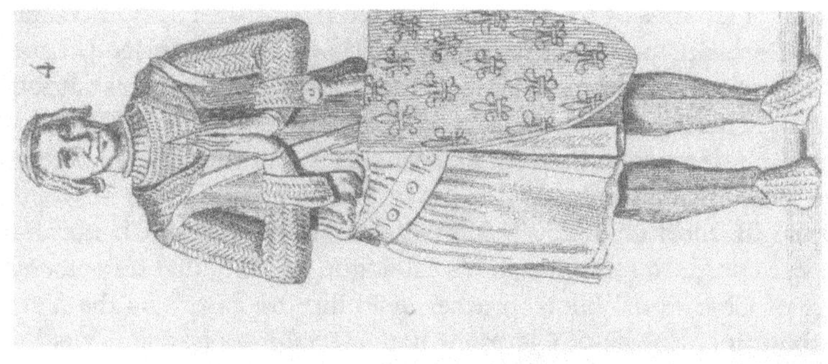

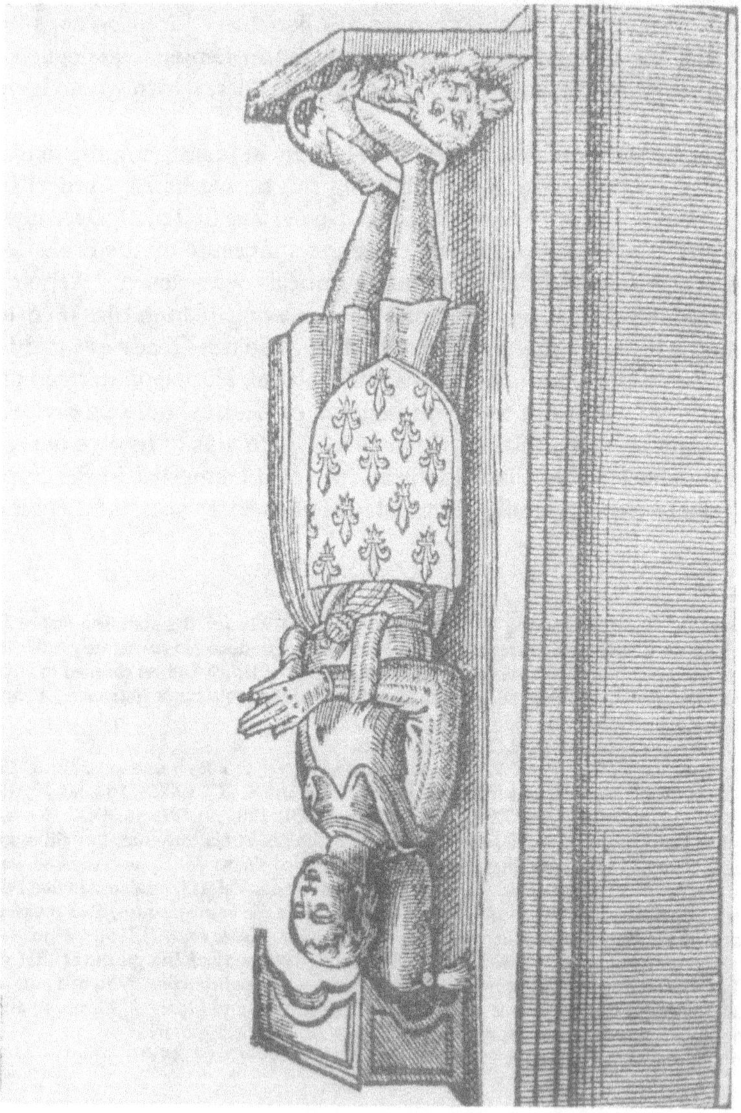

PLATE 10. Effigy of Charles of Valois. a) Jean Rabel, in Corrozet, *Antiqvitez* 2: fol. 90, and b) Millin, *Antiquités nationales*, 4: art. XXXIX, pl. 6, no. 4, facing 51. (Photographic Credit: Elizabeth A. R. Brown; New York Public Library, Rare Book Room; Avery Architectural and Fine Arts Library, Columbia University)

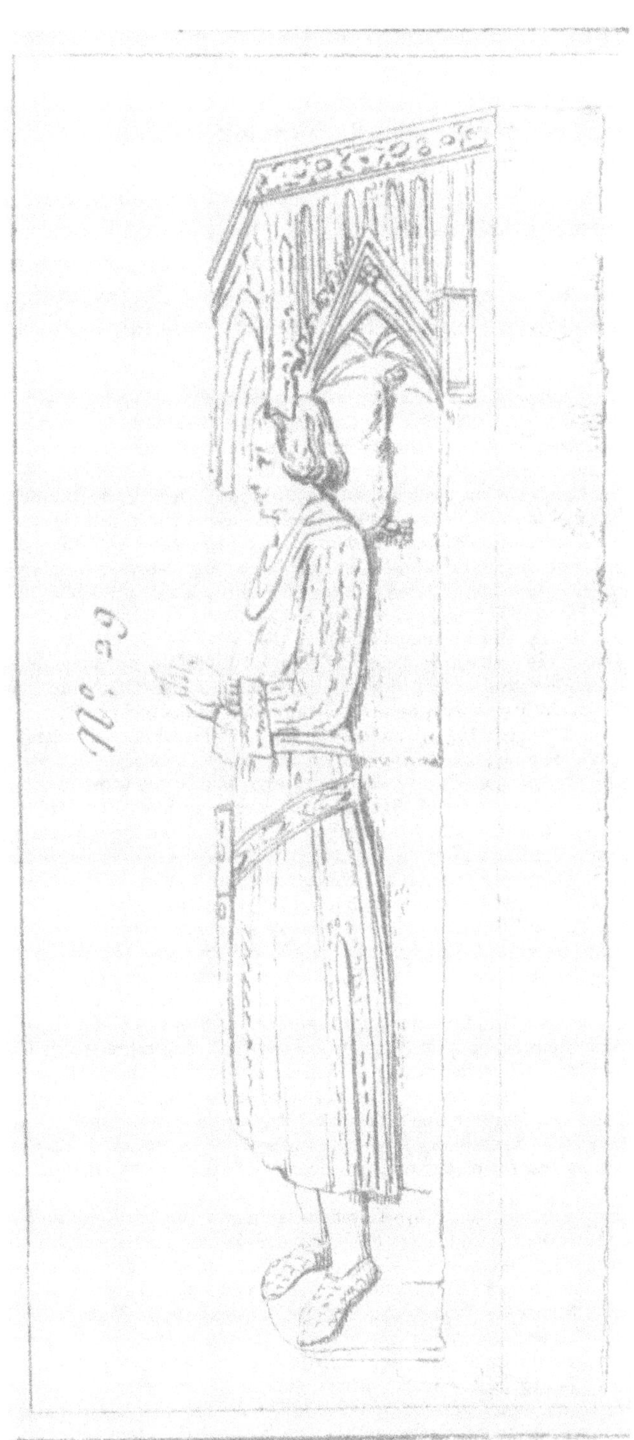

PLATE 11. Effigy of "Robert, comte de Clermont, fils de Louis IX, premier de la branche des Bourbons" (Charles of Valois). Lenoir, *Musée* 1: pl. 33, no. 29, facing 204. (Photographic Credit: Elizabeth A. R. Brown; Avery Architectural and Fine Arts Library, Columbia University)

efforts to put a halt to these projects were successful.[32] He was not so fortunate in 1816. The funerary monuments he possessed at the Petits-Augustins were in 1817 and 1818 sent from Paris to Saint-Denis. Although he was named supervisor of monuments at the abbey church, Lenoir exercised little influence and gradually faded into retirement.[33]

The architect in charge of Saint-Denis was François Debret. Having succeeded Jacques Cellerier in 1813, he adopted and elaborated on the plans his predecessor had devised in 1811 for the installation of royal funerary monuments in the crypt of Saint-Denis. The aim of the enterprise was to create there a complete record of the rulers of France from Clovis, the first Christian king, to Louis XVIII (plate 12). Authentic monuments of

---

[32] Guilhermy, *Monographie,* 101–102; *Inventaire général des richesses,* 3: 136–37, no. CCCCLXI, and cf. 1: 406, no. CCCCXXVI for Lenoir's report of 2 April 1811 to the Emperor regarding the monuments in his museum. For Napoleon's plans, see Roger van Lancker, "Napoléon et l'abbaye de Saint-Denis," *Revue de l'Institut Napoléon* 70 (1959): 97–100; and Jean-Marie Jenn, "La restauration des tombeaux (1813–1846)," in Erlande-Brandenburg et al., *Le roi, la sculpture et la mort,* 55–56; "Coup-d'oeil historique sur la ville de Saint-Denis . . . ," *Recueil polytechnique des Ponts et Chaussées* 2, 10e cahier (1807): 145–56; and particularly AN, F[13] 203, Liasse "Eglise de Sainte-Geneviève," for Napoleon's own intentions for Saint-Denis, recorded in notes he dictated in a meeting of the Conseil des Ministres on 12 February 1806; AN, F[13] 1293, Liasse "Direction de l'architecte Legrand," particularly the letters dated 9 May, 19 July, and 23 August 1806; see also AN, F[21] 1451, Debret, 5, who says that Napoleon ordered the restoration of Saint-Denis "peut-être un peu pour rattacher sa dynastie à celle de Charlemagne." Plans for the transformation of the church into an imperial mausoleum were apparently spurred when Napoleon visited Saint-Denis on 5 August 1811. Three days later, on 8 August 1811, Lenoir, protesting all the while, submitted a list of monuments that could be transferred to Saint-Denis and Sainte-Geneviève: AN, F[17A] 1280A, Dossier 7 of Liasse "3e Division, Bureau des Beaux-Arts, Musée des Monuments français 1811." In accordance with the decree of 1811, Jacques Cellerier, architect of Saint-Denis from 1808–13, prepared an elaborate plan for installing in the crypt the monuments from the Petits-Augustins and other memorials. In 1814, after succeeding Cellerier, François Debret reviewed this plan and prepared a similar but even more elaborate one: ADP, Album Debret, Caveaux no. 22 (no. 5794) and Caveaux no. 23 (no. 5795); Ferdinand, Baron de Guilhermy, and Charles Fichot, *L'église impériale de Saint-Denis et ses tombeaux, par les auteurs de la Monographie de Saint-Denis* (Paris: Charles Fichot, 1867), 6–7. See also AN, F[13] 1295 ("Eglise abbatiale de St. Denis, 1811–1822"), no. 142, a list of funerary monuments at Lenoir's museum to be restored to Saint-Denis, compiled by François Debret and dated 22 January 1816. See also ibid., letters to and from Alexandre Lenoir dated 8 and 10 May 1816; the report of 22 March 1816 on the progress of restoration; and (no. 120) the protest which Alexandre Lenoir addressed to M. le Chevalier Bruyères, Maître des Requêtes, Direction générale des travaux publics de Paris, which refers to a letter addressed to the king (printed, with additions in Lenoir's hand, and also found in this carton) pleading for the maintenance of the Musée des monumens français as a repository for the monuments which could not be restored to their original locations and for plaster casts of those which were to be removed from the Petits-Augustins.

[33] See the biography of Lenoir in Jean-Chrétien-Ferdinand Hoefer, *Nouvelle biographie générale,* 46 vols. (Paris: Firmin Didot, 1852–68), 30: 673–74; the obituary of Lenoir by M. Allou, "Notice sur la vie et les travaux d'Alexandre Lenoir," *Mémoires de la Société nationale des antiquaires de France* n.s., 6 (1842): xviii–xix; Bruno Foucart, "La fortune d'Alexandre Lenoir et du premier Musée des monuments français," *Information de l'histoire de l'art* 14e année, 5 (1969): 223–32; and Geneviève Bresc–Bautier, "Tombeaux factices de l'abbatiale de Saint–Denis ou l'art d'accommoder les restes," *Bulletin de la Société nationale des antiquaires de France* (1980–81): 114–16. See also *Inventaire général des richesses,* 3: 156–62, no. CCCCLXXIX, 286–92, no. DIX; Courajod, 1: 179–81; AN, F[21] 1451, Debret, 21; and Jacques Vanuxem, "Aperçus sur quelques tableaux représentant la Musée des Monuments français de Lenoir," *Bulletin de la Société de l'art français* (1921): 149–50.

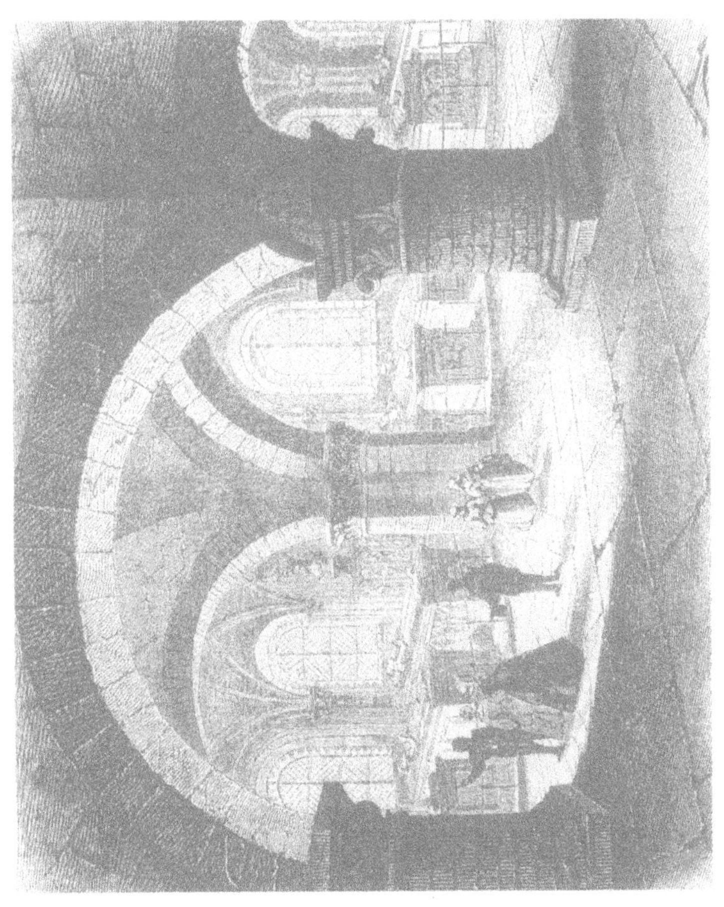

PLATE 12. Tombs in the crypt of Saint-Denis. F. Thorigny, Paris, Bibliothèque nationale, Cabinet des estampes, B 13783. (Photographic Credit: Paris, Bibliothèque nationale)

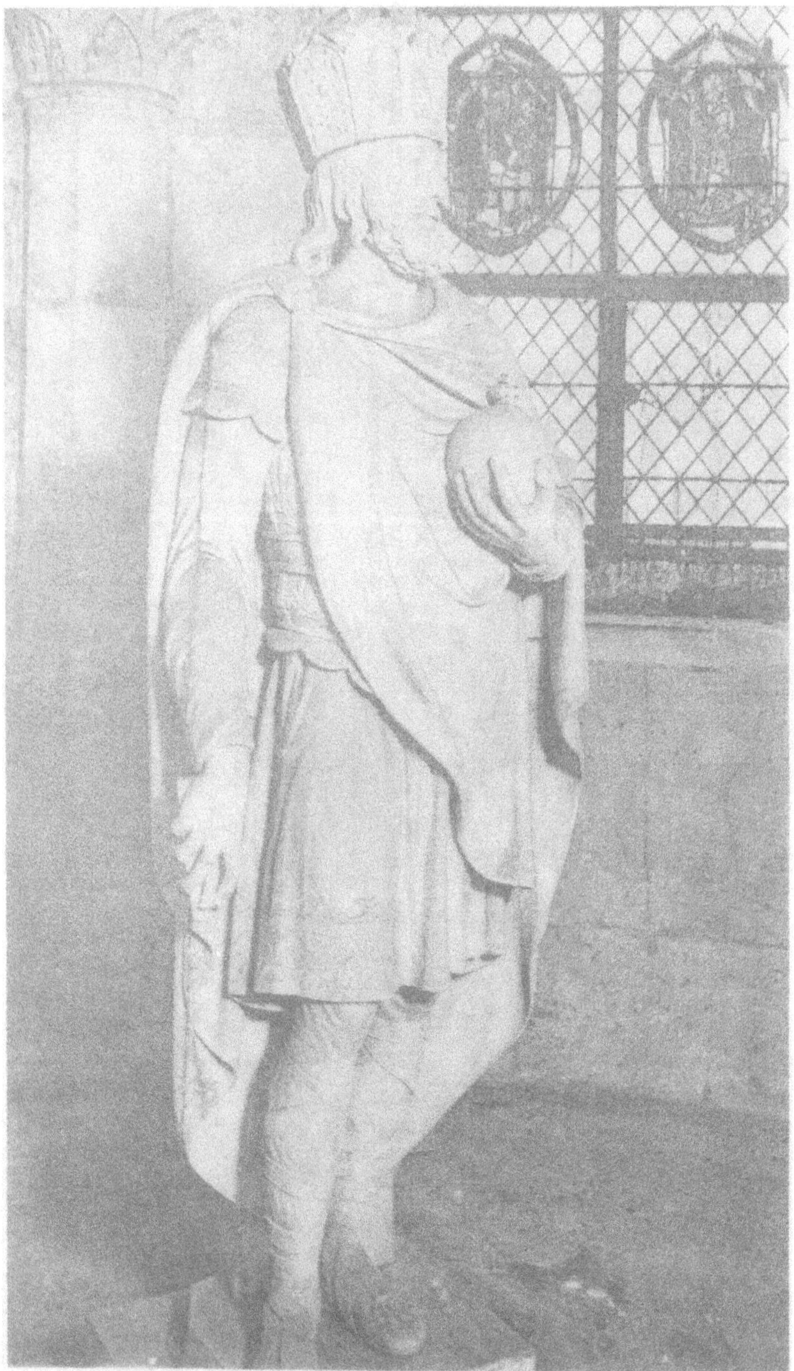

PLATE 13. Statue of Charlemagne in the crypt of Saint-Denis. (Photographic Credit: Elizabeth A. R. Brown; Musée de l'Ile-de-France, Sceaux)

the past were preferred, but when these were lacking, reproductions and modern statues, such as those Napoleon had had made of his imperial predecessors (plate 13),[34] were employed.

According to Debret, only a few definitive installations of monuments were made before the late 1830s. It is, however, noteworthy that the budgets of 1827 and 1833 for Saint-Denis included sums for restoring the monuments and for the "restauration et pose de 45 statues et sarcophages."[35] Whatever the extent of Debret's work in the crypt, he misidentified a number of the monuments housed there. Many of these mistakes were noted by Guilhermy, who apparently began visiting Saint-Denis in 1833. In his journal he carefully recorded Debret's accomplishments and, with some relish, the errors which Debret made.[36]

Guilhermy's visits to Saint-Denis brought him into direct contact with Debret, then thirty-one years his senior. By 1838 Debret was consulting Guilhermy about his projects at Saint-Denis, and particularly about the monuments housed in the crypt; the two men apparently worked together on the project between 1838 or 1839 and 1840. On 27 June 1840 Denis Destors, an architect who assisted Debret at Saint-Denis, wrote Guilhermy to tell him that on the next day Debret was to begin "la confrontation des figures des caveaux de St. Denis, muni de tous les renseignements nécessaires et du Montfaucon." He emphasized that Guilhermy's presence would be extremely useful for "une investigation dont il a lui même dirigé les premières recherches."[37] Thus Guilhermy must bear some of the responsibility for the misidentifications that were made, even though in later years—and particularly after Debret was forced to leave Saint-Denis in 1846 and Viollet-le-Duc and Guilhermy replaced him[38]—Guilhermy became Debret's outspoken critic.[39]

---

[34] Guilhermy and Fichot, *Eglise impériale,* 32; for the statue of Charlemagne at Saint-Denis, see *Inventaire général des richesses,* 3: 157, no. 17, no. CCCCLXXIX; see also "Coup-d'oeil historique," 153–54; and AN, F^{21} 1451, Debret, 8, 10–12, 18, 24, 28–29. See also ibid., 24 and AN, F^{13} 1295 for Debret's proposal (21 February 1817) to install other tombs from Lenoir's museum in the so-called Cimetière des Valois on the north side of the church. For the opening of the crypt on 24 October 1824, see AN, F^{21} 1451, Debret, 33.

[35] ADP, SSDB, Dossier 1841–76, fol. 33v, and Guilhermy, BN, n.a.f. 6121, fol. 14v; Jenn, "Restauration," 57. In 1838 more than thirty monuments awaited placement in the crypt, and many memorials had been only provisionally installed there: J.-A. Dulaure, *Histoire physique, civile et morale des environs de Paris depuis les premiers temps historiques jusqu'à nos jours. . . ,* 2nd ed., ed. J.-L. Belin, 6 vols. (Paris: Furne, 1838), 2: 251–52.

[36] For Guilhermy's visits to Saint-Denis, see BN, n.a.f. 6121, fol. 14v (1833), 17 (1838), 17v (1839), 18 (1840), 19 (1841).

[37] Guilhermy, BN, n.a.f., fol. 163, included with Guilhermy's notes. Debret's reports for 1838 and 1843 contain references to the restoration of the tombs: AN, F^{13} 528A and B.

[38] Guilhermy, BN, n.a.f. 6121, fol. 22; ADP, SSDB, Dossier 1841–76, fols. 84–86, 89–90; and ADP, SSDB, Correspondance administrative 1836–1851 (hereafter ADP, SSDB, CA 1836–51), fols. 110–111.

[39] In 1844 Guilhermy wrote an article attacking Debret's work which was published anonymously under the title "Saint-Denys. Restauration de l'église royale," in *Annales archéologiques* 1 (1844): 230–36. Didron aîné, who reported Guilhermy's authorship of the article, said that Guilhermy had refused to have a second part published because he was moved "par la vieillesse et les bonnes intentions de M. Debret": Didron, "Flèche de Saint-Denis," *Annales archéologiques* 4 (1846): 178. The second part of Guilhermy's article was in fact published, under his name, in 1846: "Restauration de l'église royale de Saint-Denis," *Annales archéologiques* 5 (1846): 200–15.

The serious work of identifying the funerary monuments commenced, according to Debret, in 1838, according to Guilhermy, in 1839.[40] Debret was sure enough of his research to have incised on the slabs and bases, in Gothic letters, the identifications that were proposed, a process which continued from 1839 to the spring of 1841 (plate 14).[41] Alexandre Lenoir,

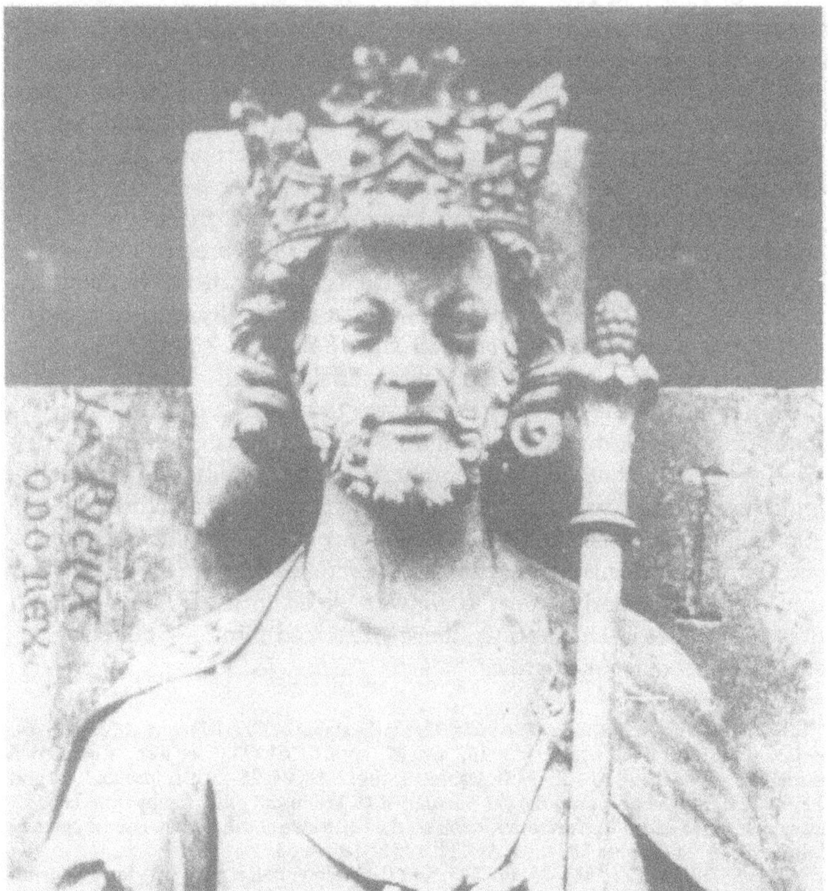

PLATE 14. Effigy of "Odo" (Robert the Pious). Fichot, "Tombeaux," Paris, Bibliothèque nationale, Cabinet des estampes, Pe 12a, no. 13. (Photographic Credit: Elizabeth A. R. Brown, and Paris, Bibliothèque nationale)

---

[40] ADP, SSDB, Dossier 1841–76, fols. 33v, 142v–43; Guilhermy, BN, n.a.f. 6121, fol. 17v; n.a.f. 6122, pp. 190–91; Guilhermy and Fichot, *Eglise impériale,* 31. See notes 46, 56, 60, and 62 below. For another aspect of Debret's work on the crypt, see Bresc-Bautier, "Tombeaux factices," 114–27.

[41] Guilhermy, BN, n.a.f. 6121, fols. 17–18, 19, 164, 181; and his *Monographie,* 215, where he dates the work 1840–41. For a record of many of the inscriptions, see Guilhermy, BN, n.a.f. 6121, fols. 176v–83v. The slab inscriptions were generally carefully modeled on the original inscriptions, recorded in pre-Revolutionary works, but those on the bases were Debret's own inventions. Thus, for example, Robert the Pious was identified as "Robertus rex" on the slab and as "Robert (le pieux) mort en 1031" on his sarcophagus: ibid., fol. 181v. For comments on the armorial devices with which some monuments were decorated, see a note made on 30 July 1847, in ibid., fol. 200. Another list of inscriptions, compiled by Guilhermy, is found in Guilhermy, BN, n.a.f. 6122, fols. 205–32, where he carefully distinguished authentic inscriptions from modern ones.

who might have aided in the work, died on 11 June 1839. Whether, at the end of his life, he would have given completely sound advice is unclear, for a work of his that was published posthumously in 1840 identified the gisant of Carloman as Charles Martel's.[42]

According to Debret's memorandum of 14 January 1842, the work proceeded systematically. The sources that were used represented the best available. They ranged from the well-known pre-Revolutionary books on Paris and the royal lineage—those of Bonfons, Du Breul, Doublet, Millet, Félibien, Montfaucon, Millin, Anselme, and Lebeuf—to two unpublished collections at the Bibliothèque royale and a manuscript of the account of the exhumations of 1793 written by Germain Poirier. One of the collections at the royal library was the "grand portefeuille de Gagnières [sic]," doubtless the collection of drawings of the royal tomb figures in life-like poses that had been employed by Montfaucon. Debret also set in motion investigations in England that led to the rediscovery of the Gaignières drawings at Oxford. These he almost surely never saw, but he did receive from his English agent a series of engravings of funerary monuments at the Cordeliers and the Jacobins executed by Thomas Kerrich in 1785 and based on drawings Kerrich had made in the early 1770s.[43]

Debret asserted in 1842 that eleven previously misdesignated monuments had been correctly identified, and the notes of Guilhermy support his statement.[44] It is not surprising that Debret claimed credit for the work, or that Guilhermy said that he was responsible for the successes. Errors had indeed abounded, nor were they all remedied. In 1847 Guilhermy roundly condemned the arrangement of monuments in the crypt as "une fantaisie matrimoniale des plus bizarres," as the work of a "digne personnage" who "ne recula ni devant l'adultère, ni même devant l'inceste." According to Guilhermy, "par suite d'erreurs fortuites ou volontaires," a number of tombs bore incorrect designations: Berthe, for example, was said to be Hermentrude, and Hermentrude, Berthe; Carloman (I?) was identified as Henri I, Catherine of Courtenay as Blanche of Castile, and—a transformation that would have given the principals pause—Louis of Evreux as Charles of Valois. To produce Louis of Evreux, the effigy of his son, Charles of Etampes, had been called into service.[45]

---

[42] Alexandre Lenoir, *Monumens des arts libéraux, mécaniques et industriels de la France, depuis les Gaulois jusqu'au règne de François Ier* (Paris: J. Techener, 1840), pl. XIX and p. 13; cf. his *Musée*, 1: pl. 26, no. 11.

[43] ADP, SSDB, Dossier 1841–76, fol. 34v. Debret's reference to "ces précieux documents qui me furent envoyés" and which were "parfaitement d'accord avec mes recherches historiques" in all likelihood applies only to the Kerrich drawings. On the early guides to Paris which Debret said he consulted, see Maurice Dumolin, "Notes sur les vieux guides de Paris," *Mémoires de la Société de l'histoire de Paris et de l'Ile-de-France* 47 (1924): 209–85. How closely Debret studied the works he cited is unclear; see AN, F^{21} 1451, Debret, 2 for his reference to "Philibien." On Kerrich, see Appendix II.

[44] ADP, SSDB, Dossier 1841–76, fols. 34v, 143; Guilhermy, BN, n.a.f. 6121, fols. 160v–224.

[45] ADP, SSDB, Dossier 1841–76, fols. 38v, 142v; see also Guilhermy, BN, n.a.f. 6121, fols. 17v, 174, 176v, 180, 192, 195; Guilhermy, *Monographie*, 106–8, 272–74, and his third plan, a diagram of the crypt showing the placement of monuments there. This plan appears to have been based on one drawn by Debret, entitled "Traveaux [sic] Exécutés dans les caveaux de l'Eglise Royale de St Denis conformément à l'ordonnance du Roi en date du 24 avril 1816," CRMH, Dessins Viollet-le-Duc, no. 8079 (MH 203696), published under the erroneous date

Guilhermy later stated that his advice, based on a study of Montfaucon's plates, led to the correct identification of the effigies of Berthe and Hermentrude before false inscriptions could be incised on their monuments. In 1840 he was able to rectify (as he believed) the incorrect designation of Catherine of Courtenay as Blanche of Castile. Owing to his intervention, he said, the monuments of Charles of Alençon and his wife Marie were reunited—Charles's effigy had been in storage, whereas Marie's had been wrongly identified as Jeanne of Burgundy, wife of Philip V. He also took credit for restoring their proper identities to the gisants of Louis of Evreux and Charles of Valois, and thus for determining that the gisant said to be Robert of Clermont's (in fact Charles of Valois's) could not be his. In the process, the gisant of Charles of Etampes recovered its true identity.[46]

According to Guilhermy, Debret was particularly reluctant to alter the designation of the gisant of "Robert of Clermont," the identity Lenoir had first assigned to the effigy of Charles of Valois. He did not want to deprive Saint-Denis of a representation, apocryphal or not, of the chief of the Bourbon line, especially since Louis Philippe, when visiting Saint-Denis, had paid particular attention to the tomb. His hand was forced, however, by an engraving by Thomas Kerrich, sent to him from England, which depicted the gisant of Charles of Valois in great detail (plate 15).[47]

Guilhermy's account is hardly fair. Since Debret had initiated the research that produced Kerrich's engravings, the credit for correcting this error—and thus for identifying correctly the tombs of Louis of Evreux and Charles of Etampes—is in fact Debret's.[48] It should, on the other hand, be noted that, like Lenoir, both Debret and Guilhermy could have identified these tombs, without benefit of Kerrich's engraving, from readily available sources.[49]

1816 in Jules Formigé, *L'abbaye royale de Saint-Denis. Recherches nouvelles* (Paris: Presses universitaires de la France, 1960), fig. 167, facing 184; the tomb of the son of the duc de Berry, who died in 1818, is indicated on the plan, and the works are said to have been "exécutés" rather than simply projected; it thus seems likely to have been drawn in 1840 or 1841. See also AN, F[21] 1451, Debret, Dessin 1 (1832) ("Plan général des caveaux"), and the key to the drawing, [49]. See 30 below.

[46] Guilhermy, BN, n.a.f. 6121, fols. 17v, 159–v, 174, 176v, 185v, 192, 195–v, 202; on fol. 17v Guilhermy suggests that all these rectifications were made "vers le mois de Juillet" in 1839, but, as his other notes show, this could not have been the case. It is possible that his involvement with the work commenced at that time.

[47] Guilhermy, BN, n.a.f. 6121, fol. 195v, and, for Guilhermy's placement of the tomb, fols. 147v and 151; see also AN, F[21] 1451, Debret, [49v], no. 60. See, too, a letter of Debret dated 25 July 1837 which mentions the king's visit to Saint-Denis and also notes the necessity of accomplishing "Le placement dans la Crypte Souterraine de la Suite des figures ou tombes Royales qui sont dans nos ateliers de St Denis." For Didron's attack on the window which Debret installed in the crossing of Saint-Denis in honor of Louis Philippe's visit in 1837, see Didron, "Flèche de Saint-Denis," 180; cf. Guilhermy, "Restauration," 213.

[48] In his own report of 14 January 1842, Debret reported the incident without comment: ADP, SSDB, Dossier 1841–76, fol. 34v.

[49] For Charles of Valois, see n. 28 above. The monument of Louis of Evreux, who was also buried at the church of the Jacobins, was reproduced in Millin's article on the church, although it was not identified in the text (Millin, *Antiquités nationales*, 4: art. XXXIX, pl. 8, no. 2, facing 82, and cf. 77–78; see also Hennin, 4: 237); it was, however, depicted and identified in Montfaucon, 2: pl. XXXVIII, no. 2; for drawings of this monument in the Gaignières collection, see Adhémar, "Tombeaux," no. 624. A depiction of the tomb of Robert of Clermont appears in Montfaucon, 2: pl. XXVII, no. 10; cf. 161–62; his monument was drawn a

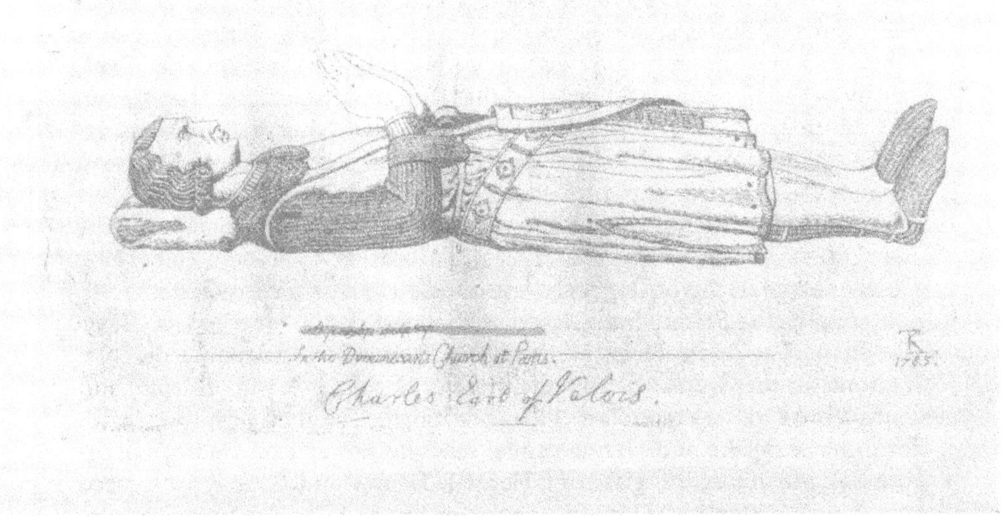

PLATE 15. Effigy of Charles of Valois. Engraving by Thomas Kerrich, 1785. (Photographic Credit: Elizabeth A. R. Brown, by courtesy of the Trustees of Sir John Soane's Museum and Architectural Library)

In fact neither Guilhermy nor Debret was fully conversant with the books and pictures which Debret said were used when the revised identifications were made. Guilhermy later commented that, in the spring of 1841, Charles Martel was through his effigy's inscription accorded the quality of king "qu'on avait long temps tardé à lui donner." His sarcasm should have been directed, not against Debret, but rather, in the spirit of Félibien, against those who originally labeled the effigy. Anyone familiar with the pre-Revolutionary works on Saint-Denis would have known full well that Charles Martel's monument had, since its creation, borne this title.[50] Whatever the intent of Guilhermy's remark, it is clear that, had he and Debret worked meticulously between 1839 and 1841, many mistakes that remained might have been avoided. Correct epitaphs were given, for example, to only half of the sixteen effigies created for Saint-Denis in the 1260s.

Of the sixteen Dyonisian monuments created in the 1260s, two had disappeared by the time the group was restored to Saint-Denis. In 1801 Lenoir stated that the tombs of both Henri I and Louis VI had been destroyed in 1793, and none of his subsequent catalogues or inventories indicates that he possessed either monument. His records, however, reveal

---

number of times for Gaignières: Adhémar, "Tombeaux," nos. 618, 723; Bouchot, nos. 237, 4457, 4510, 4805. As has been seen (see notes 23 and 28 above), Lenoir correctly identified the tomb of Charles of Etampes, and he seems to have been aware of the true identity of the gisant of Charles of Valois. For Kerrich's drawings and engravings of these tombs, see Appendix II.

[50] Guilhermy, BN, n.a.f. 6121, fol. 17v–18; Félibien, 39–40, 551; Montfaucon, 1: 272.

that on 13 February 1795 he indeed received the effigy of Henri I.[51] Since the gisants of Eudes and Hugues Capet had been at the Petits-Augustins when Lenoir's museum was dissolved, Debret—and presumably Guilhermy as well—apparently believed that they must still exist. They had in fact disappeared, and the effigies of Henri I and of Louis VI, long missing, had somehow come to light. Nonetheless, to produce the Eudes and Hugues Capet that were presumed needed, the effigies of Robert and Louis VI assumed the identities of their ancestors. Clovis III, son of Louis the Stammerer, became Robert, and Clovis's brother Carloman II became Clovis. Clovis II, son of Dagobert, was pressed into service as Carloman II, son of Louis the Stammerer. Carloman I, son of Pepin, emerged as Clovis II, son of Dagobert. Thus, according to Debret's calculations, the two monuments that were missing were those of Carloman I, son of Pepin, and Louis VI. As to the eight correct identifications, Guilhermy claimed credit for those of Berthe and Hermentrude, whereas he rejected Debret's accurate designation of the gisant of Henri I. Debret and Guilhermy agreed regarding the identities of five monuments: those of Charles Martel, Pepin, Philip I, and the two Queens Constance.[52]

When Guilhermy prepared extensive notes on the funerary monuments in the crypt of Saint-Denis, probably after his official association with the abbey in 1846,[53] he still insisted that the actual effigy of Henri I was that of Carloman I, son of Pepin, and he accepted four of the misidentifications of the effigies of the 1260s made between 1839 and 1841—those of the gisants of Carloman, son of Pepin (as Clovis II, son of Dagobert), of Robert (as Eudes), of Louis VI[54] (as Hugues Capet), and of Clovis III, son of Louis the Stammerer (as Robert). Guilhermy had realized that the effigy wrongly designated as Clovis, son of Louis the Stammerer, was in fact that of

---

[51] Courajod, 1: 21, no. 166; 77–78, no. 532; 80, no. 556; 90, no. 616; 96, nos. 667, 670; 104, no. 730; *Inventaire général des richesses,* 1: 14–15, no. XVII; 406, no. CCCCXXVI; 2: 78, no. LXII; 218–19, no. CLXI; 231–32, no. CLXXVI; 387, 390–91; 3: 246, no. XDII, section 26; Lenoir, *Musée,* 2: xxv, xxxviii. Erlande-Brandenburg indicates that neither the effigy of Henri I nor that of Louis VI was ever lost but, rather, that both monuments were taken to the Petits-Augustins under the guises of Eudes and Hugues Capet and were in 1817 restored to the abbey: Erlande-Brandenburg, *Le roi,* 159–60, nos. 78, 83, and cf. 158, nos. 71–72, n. 1; see n. 12 above. This theory seems implausible in view of the evident similarities between Lenoir's depictions of the effigies of Eudes and Hugues Capet (fig. 3) and the images of these tombs preserved in the works of Félibien and Montfaucon (fig. 5), and in the Gaignières drawings used by Montfaucon (fig. 4): Lenoir, *Musée,* 1: pl. 27, nos. 15–16, facing 186; Félibien, pl. facing 550; Montfaucon, 1: pls. XXIX, facing 306, and XXXIII, facing 370; for the Gaignières drawings, BN, RE, Oa 9, fols. 19, 21. Comparison with the figures in Félibien's engraving of the tombs of the crossing reveals that the identifying inscriptions of the two Gaignières drawings, faithfully reproduced by Montfaucon, are reversed. The figure on the left should be Eudes, that on the right Hugues Capet: see figs. 17–18.

[52] Traces of the incorrect inscriptions can still be discerned on the tombs: see the photographs in Erlande-Brandenburg, *Le roi,* plates XXXV–XLII; cf. Guilhermy, BN, n.a.f. 6121, fols. 131v, 174, 176v, 180, 182. See also fig. 14 and n. 41 above.

[53] Guilhermy, BN, n.a.f. 6121, fols. 160v–224, and see particularly fols. 162, 164, 173v, and 200.

[54] The statue identified as Louis VI in the crypt was, according to Guilhermy, a plaster statue made ca. 1817; Guilhermy, BN, n.a.f. 6121, fol. 182v; see also 131v, 136; n.a.f. 6122, p. 216.

Clovis's brother Carloman II. He introduced an additional problem, however, by asserting that the gisant identified as Carloman II, son of Louis the Stammerer (actually that of Clovis II, son of Dagobert), was that of the Clovis III who was Carloman II's brother, son of Louis the Stammerer. The opinions recorded in his notes Guilhermy published in the *Monographie de l'église royale de Saint-Denis* which, announced in 1847, appeared the following year.[55]

Thus, in 1841 confusion still reigned in the crypt of Saint-Denis. Some correct identifications had indeed been made. Since Debret's mistakes outweighed his successes, however, he was hardly immune from attack. In 1841 an anonymous report, attributed to "Comte X" and entitled "Observations critiques sur la restauration de l'Eglise Royale de St Denis," dwelled at length on his erroneous and misleading labels.[56] The members of the Commission des monuments historiques who visited Saint-Denis on 10 June 1841 concluded that only a special report would be sufficient to detail all the mistakes perpetrated in the crypt.[57] Their visit led to the preparation of an official report, sent by the Ministre de l'Intérieur (Direction des Beaux-Arts) to the Ministre des Travaux publics on 19 October 1841. Referring to the monuments as "ces archives mortuaires de la Royauté," the report called for the rectification of the misidentifications.[58] The Ministre des Travaux publics forwarded the anonymous "Observations critiques" to both the Académie des Inscriptions et Belles-Lettres and the Académie des Beaux-Arts, which named a joint, seven-member committee to consider the report. On 20 November the committee determined to send to Debret for his consideration an excerpted copy (excluding "toutes les expressions qui pouvaient affliger un artiste aussi recommend-

---

[55] Guilhermy, *Monographie*, 213–32, with reversed captions on 222 (cf. 223); see also his "Monographie de l'église royale de Saint-Denis. Tombeaux et figures historiques," *Annales archéologiques* 7 (1847): 297–302; and Guilhermy, BN, n.a.f. 6121, fols. 131v, 178. See n. 119 below.

[56] This report is included as an *annexe* in ADP, SSDB, CA 1836–51. It consists of six folios, and the inscriptions are discussed on fol. 4. Note particularly the marginal note on fol. 4v: "Le nombre de fausses inscriptions, répandues dans tout le monument, l'ignorance et l'affectation qui ont présidé au choix de ces monuments, font de cette partie de la restauration de St. Denis une des choses les plus humiliantes pour la sincérité, la science et le bon sens du pays."

[57] ADP, SSDB, Dossier 1841–76, fol. 6v, where similar comments were made regarding the stained glass of the church. Meetings of the Commission on 14 and 21 June considered the work of Debret: ADP, SSDB, CA 1836–51, fol. 1 and 5bis of the *annexe* referred to in the preceding note; see also *Les premiers travaux de la Commission des monuments historiques 1837–1848*, ed. Françoise Bercé (Bibliothèque de la Sauvegarde de l'art français; Paris: A. et J. Picard, 1979), 150–52, and also 213–14 for a meeting on 3 June 1842 at which Debret was also discussed.

[58] The report concluded, "C'est surtout dans les caveaux où sont conservés les tombeaux de nos Rois, qu'une révision sévère des inscriptions nous semblera sans doute indispensable. Il paraît qu'une étrange méthode a présidé à leur composition. Lorsqu'on manquait de renseignements positifs sur une statue, au lieu d'avouer qu'elle représentait un personnage inconnu, on lui a donné un nom, non pas même sous forme d'hypothèse, mais avec assurance et en se servant de lettres gothiques pour mieux surprendre la crédulité du lecteur. De semblables fictions peuvent-elles être tolererés [sic] dans un tel lieu? Il en est de ces archives mortuaires de la Royauté comme des registres de l'état civil, le gouvernement est responsable de leur sincérité et ne peut laisser sciemment s'y introduire des altérations": ADP, SSDB, Dossier 1841–76, fol. 9.

able").[59] Debret drafted a lengthy reply, dated 14 January 1842, a reply to which, in its report of 8 April 1842, the joint committee accorded a mixed reception.

In the end Debret was permitted to continue his work,[60] and no immediate remedy ensued. Indeed Debret's critics were, on this point, not fully agreed as to what should be done.[61] Nonetheless, Debret's reply again brought to the notice of those concerned with the monuments lodged at Saint-Denis—as well as others—the Oxford collection of drawings executed for Gaignières.[62] According to his own account, written in 1842, he had established contact in the course of his research with an English antiquarian who was commissioned to explore relevant material in the libraries of London and Oxford.[63] At Oxford Debret's researcher came upon "un portefeuille et manuscrit intitulé: des figures et tombes Royales de france." It was believed at Oxford, said Debret, that the collection "est l'original des gravures de Montfaucon et du portefeuille de Guegnère [sic]." In the Oxford collection, Debret noted, were fifteen volumes devoted to tombs, which Gough had left to Oxford; they were thought to have been acquired in France during the Revolution. He also mentioned the engravings of tombs at the Jacobins and the Cordeliers, made by Thomas Kerrich, which he had received from England.[64] These would all

[59] ADP, SSDB, CA 1836–51, fol. 19.

[60] ADP, SSDB, Dossier 1841–76, fols. 13bis-62; see also CA 1836–51, fol. 32 for Debret's letter to the Ministre des Travaux publics dated 23 May 1842, and the address which he delivered in May 1842 before a meeting of the Cinq Académies, in *Institut royal de France, Séance publique des Cinq Académies* (May, 1842): 11–28, particularly 19–21. Guilhermy reports that a commission charged with reviewing the inscriptions at Saint-Denis was named in January 1843: Guilhermy, BN, n.a.f. 6121, fol. 20v. See also Guilhermy, in *Annales archéologiques* 1 (1844): 231–32; on the inscriptions, see the second part of this article, in *Annales archéologiques* 5 (1846): 214–15. See as well Jenn, "Restauration," 58, and his article in *Le "Gothique" retrouvé*, 140–41.

[61] See the report of 8 April 1842 in ADP, SSDB, Dossier 1841–76, fols. 59v–61.

[62] Louis-Jean Guenebault became so interested in the drawings that he wrote to England to learn more about them. An informant responded from London on 5 August 1844 that the collection at Oxford contained thirteen volumes, each consisting of 100 to 120 drawings. Guenebault included a notice regarding the collection in the second volume of his iconographical dictionary, published in 1845: Louis-Jean Guenebault, *Dictionnaire iconographique des monuments de l'antiquité chrétienne et du moyen âge . . .* , 2 vols. (Paris: Leleux, 1843–45), 2: 366.

[63] If Guilhermy was correct in saying that the tomb of Charles of Valois was identified in 1839, Debret's inquiries must have been made in 1838 or 1839: Guilhermy, BN, n.a.f. 6121, fol. 195-v.

[64] ADP, SSDB, Dossier 1841–76, fol. 34v. Guilhermy's account of this discovery, presented in a report of 21 May 1847, is different from Debret's, recorded in 1842; it gives far less credit to Debret than Debret claimed and seems on the whole untrustworthy. According to Guilhermy, Debret was presented with engravings based on the drawings in the Oxford volumes, which were brought to Paris by the English engraver who had executed them. Guilhermy does not mention Thomas Kerrich, who died in 1838 and thus could not have traveled to France in 1839. Guilhermy could hardly be referring to a second set of engravings, different from those of Kerrich, since he himself insisted on the importance to Debret of the engraving of the tomb of Charles of Valois, whose effigy does not appear in the Oxford volumes: Guilhermy, BN, n.a.f. 6122, p. 192; ADP, SSDB, Dossier 1841–76, fols. 143–44; see Adhémar, "Tombeaux," no. 657 for the Gaignières drawing of Charles of Valois's effigy in BN, Clairambault 333, fol. 317.

be put to good use when Debret was replaced by Viollet-le Duc and Guilhermy. In the end, however, it was not the inscriptions on the effigies that caused Debret's departure from Saint-Denis. Rather, as Guilhermy remarked on 30 July 1847, "il fallait la chute de la flèche" for Debret to be removed and true reform at Saint-Denis to commence.[65]

---

[65] Guilhermy, BN, n.a.f. 6121, fol. 200. See also Didron, aîné, "L'église royale de Saint-Denis," *Annales archéologiques* 6 (1847): 62–63. Didron (ibid., 61) was incensed that in 1847 Debret was serving on the committee supervising the restoration of the Sainte-Chapelle; the architect died in 1850. On Debret's career and his associates at Saint-Denis, see Flamand-Grétry, *Description complète,* 252–55.

II. THE GAIGNIERES DRAWINGS AND THE RESTORATION OF THE ROYAL TOMBS OF FRANCE

On 21 May 1847, within a few months of his appointment as Viollet-le-Duc's iconographic adviser,[66] Guilhermy submitted a full report on the condition of the tombs of Saint-Denis. He strongly recommended the government's acquisition of tracings of the drawings in the Gaignières collection at Oxford; such tracings, he believed, should eventually be deposited at the Bibliothèque royale. Thus all doubts regarding the tombs of Saint-Denis could be resolved. Guilhermy urged, in addition, that the monuments be taken from the crypt and restored to their original positions in the church.[67] Together with his report, he apparently presented a plan and drawing by Viollet-le-Duc of the "anciennes sépultures de l'église haute." He hoped that it would convince the Ministre des Travaux publics "combien présentait de majestueux beauté la disposition des tombeaux dans toute l'étendue du choeur, et combien il serait désirable de la voir reproduite."[68]

Three days before the submission of Guilhermy's report, on 18 May 1847, Viollet-le-Duc addressed a letter to the Ministre des Travaux publics. Without attacking Debret by name, he seconded Guilhermy's plea to correct the many "erreurs dans le classement de toutes les statues baptisées tant de fois," which, he said, were inevitable after "tant de transports, de changements." He too called attention to the drawings in Oxford, and his

---

[66] On the appointment of Guilhermy, see the letter of 19 December 1846 (in which he was offered the post) and that of 5 January 1847 (in which the Ministre des Travaux publics informed Viollet-le-Duc that he had accepted the offer): ADP, SSDB, CA 1836–51, fols. 112–13; see also fol. 132. On Viollet–le–Duc, see Bruno Foucart, "Viollet–le–Duc et la restoration," in Nora et al., *La Nation,* 2: 612–49.

[67] Guilhermy, BN, n.a.f. 6122, pp. 193–96, and ADP, SSDB, Dossier 1841–76, fols. 144–47v; Jenn, "Restauration," 58–59.

[68] Guilhermy, BN, n.a.f. 6122, p. 196, and ADP, SSDB, Dossier 1841–76, fol. 147v. In his *Monographie* of 1848, Guilhermy published as his second plan a diagram of the "Ancienne disposition des tombeaux dans le choeur, dans le transept et dans les chapelles," which was modeled on Félibien (facing 550 and on 555); the third diagram, "Plan de la Crypte dans son état actuel" is closely related to Debret's plan of his own work in the crypt, on which see above, n. 45. It seems likely that the plans published by Guilhermy in 1848 resulted from his collaboration with Viollet-le-Duc and that the second diagram is a version of the one which Guilhermy submitted with his report of 1847. A similar plan, whose title refers to "l'Eglise impériale," is probably also the work of Viollet-le-Duc: BN, Cabinet des estampes, Ve 26g, 106, cliché 77G.84351. The script bears marked similarities to that of Viollet-le-Duc: ADP, SSDB, CA 1836–51, fols. 144–45; Dossier 1841–76, fol. 123; and Viollet-le-Duc's plan of the church, dated January 1860, CRMH, Dessins Viollet-le-Duc, no. 1190/6553, cliché MH 308427.

description of the collection was far fuller than Guilhermy's. Not only did Viollet-le-Duc list the general contents of the volumes, he also gave the sum total of volumes in the collection as sixteen and noted that two of them were unbound; he stated that one of the volumes contained some 233 drawings and that the others were composed of approximately a hundred drawings apiece. The drawings relating to Saint-Denis would, he said, make it possible to identify all the monuments at the abbey church. He suggested that the Ministre send to England to trace the drawings the artist and *archéologue* Henry Gérente, who, he proposed, should receive 2000 francs for the trip.[69]

On 24 July 1847 the suggestions of Viollet-le-Duc were formally transmitted to the Ministre des Travaux publics. Calling attention to the reports of Viollet-le-Duc and Guilhermy, the Maître des Requêtes, Chef de la Division des Bâtiments civils, noted the advantages that would result from having in France tracings or copies of the Oxford drawings. Gérente, he concurred, should execute this task; the copies he made should be housed at the Bibliothèque royale after they had been used at Saint-Denis. The money for Gérente's trip, he suggested, could be taken from the ministry's general budget for the year.[70] On 29 July 1847 Gérente accepted the commission. He asked for appropriate letters of introduction and said that he would leave for England on 20 August or thereabouts.[71] On 7 August the Ministre des Travaux publics wrote both to the Duc de Broglie, French ambassador to England, to tell him of Gérente's mission, and also to Gérente himself, to inform him of the steps that had been taken. Five days later Gérente pressed for a public announcement in *Le Moniteur* of his mission.[72]

During his stay in England Gérente established that the Oxford drawings had indeed formed part of the collection of Roger de Gaignières; he was, however, unable to discover precisely how Gough had obtained them. Nothing he learned in Oxford confirmed Debret's belief that Gough had secured them in France during the Revolution, although this opinion continued to be widely held.[73] Gérente discovered that, under the terms of

---

[69] ADP, SSDB, Dossier 1841–76, fols. 130–31v. For the order in which Viollet-le-Duc listed the Oxford volumes, see Appendix I below. The two unbound volumes were those now catalogued at Oxford as XIV and XV; their bindings differ from those of the other volumes, their pages are larger, and the edges of the pages are untrimmed. When Gough made his bequest, he said that fourteen volumes were "handsomely bound in folio," whereas two others were "in folio in yellowish boards": Bandinel and Bliss, *Catalogue . . . Richard Gough*, 4.

[70] ADP, SSDB, CA 1836–51, fols. 132–39, and Dossier 1851–76, fol. 178.

[71] ADP, SSDB, CA 1836–51, fol. 135.

[72] ADP, SSDB, CA 1836–51, fols. 132, 134, 138bis–39, and Dossier 1841–76, fols. 130, 144v, 152, 158; see also Guilhermy, BN, n.a.f. 6122, fol. 193; and Louis Grodecki, *Les vitraux de Saint-Denis. Etude sur le vitrail au XIIe siècle*, I (Corpus Vitrearum Medii Aevi, France, Series "Etudes," Département de Seine-Saint-Denis; Paris: Centre National de la Recherche Scientifique, Arts et Metiers graphiques, 1976), 52.

[73] See Guenebault, "Notice," 46, n. 3, and 47, who said that the collection had passed to England "par suite d'une spoliation violente faite au Cabinet des estampes à l'époque de la première révolution."

Gough's bequest, it would be virtually impossible for the French government ever to regain them. William Ewart Gladstone, then Member of Parliament for Oxford, had cautioned diplomacy in any negotiations. An exchange involving the volumes would have to be effected by a private act of Parliament, and the French government would be obliged to pay the considerable costs of such an act, which Gérente thought might amount to several hundred pounds.[74] The revolution that led to the establishment of the Second Republic in France in 1848 militated against the success of any such scheme. Nonetheless, Gérente's work at the Bodleian was successful; his stay in England also produced for him a number of commissions for work on stained glass.[75] At Oxford, the Bodleian's librarian, Bulkeley Bandinel,[76] permitted him to trace the drawings, "malgré les règlemens." Thus Gérente was able to submit a full, if not exhaustive, report on the Oxford collection. It included an inventory of the volumes and transcriptions of the epitaphs of the members of the royal lineage recorded in the first two volumes, as well as some two hundred tracings.[77]

---

[74] According to Guenebault ("Notice," 42), in February 1848 or thereabouts Gérente served as intermediary in negotiations aimed at recovering the Gaignières volumes for France.

[75] Louis-Jean Guenebault, *Dictionnaire iconographique des figures, légendes et actes des saints . . .*, vol. 45 of *Encyclopédie théologique*, ed. J.-P. Migne (Paris: J.-P. Migne, 1850), 1042–43, and *Annales archéologiques* 9 (1849): 184.

[76] On Bandinel (1781–1861), see the article by Richard Garnett in *Dictionary of National Biography* and also Edmund Craster, *History of the Bodleian Library 1845–1945* (Oxford: Clarendon Press, 1952), 26–43. On Bandinel's courtesy to the French, see Guenebault, "Notice," 52, n. 1, who wrote in 1853 that Bandinel "a toujours accueilli les archéologues français et les dessinateurs qui lui ont demandé la communication des volumes de Gaignières, qui doivent tant nous intéresser."

[77] ADP, SSDB, Dossier 1841–76, fols. 159–77. See Guenebault, "Notice," 47, 50, for the number of tracings; it was clearly from Viollet-le-Duc, who in 1853 had Gérente's tracings in his possession, that Guenebault obtained his information: ibid., 47, n. 1. I have been unable to determine whether or not these tracings still exist. Gérente's catalogue was published in 1852 in the *Bulletin du Comité historique des arts et monuments. Archéologie, Beaux-Arts* 3: 229–45, 269–88; cf. ADP, SSDB, Dossier 1841–76, fols. 161–77; see Appendix I below for a comparison of his inventory with that presented by Viollet-le-Duc on 18 May 1847 (see above following n. 68) and with the current order of the volumes at the Bodleian. Gérente's inventory evidently reflects the numeration of the volumes at the Bodleian Library while he was in Oxford; this order, found as well in the inventory subsequently prepared for Michel Hennin (see Appendix I), determined the sequence of the volumes of tracings of the Oxford drawings now housed in the Réserve des estampes at the Bibliothèque nationale. By 1897, when Madan published the fourth volume of his summary catalogue of the Western manuscripts of the Bodleian, the order of the Oxford volumes was altered; a few of the volumes bear, inside their covers, indications of their former arrangement: see Appendix I and Falconer Madan, *A Summary Catalogue of Western Manuscripts in the Bodleian Library at Oxford*, 7 vols. (Oxford: Clarendon Press, 1895–1953), 4: 295–96, nos. 18346–61. The order recorded in Gérente's inventory apparently was still in use in the early 1860s, when, as will be seen, Jules Frappaz executed his tracings. Although Frappaz did not proceed perfectly systematically with his work, he worked roughly from beginning to end. His tracings of the drawings in the volume devoted to the Ile-de-France (catalogued as the third volume in Gérente's inventory but as the twelfth volume in the current system of classification at the Bodleian) were all validated by Bandinel, who retired as Bodley's librarian in November 1860 and died on 6 February 1861. Thus they must have been completed within six months of Gérente's arrival in Oxford.

Gérente died in 1849, and his work in Oxford bore no immediate fruit at Saint-Denis. The journal of work at the church which the architect Mesnages kept between January 1847 and 19 July 1849 makes few references to the tombs, still on display in the crypt.[78] In 1853 Louis-Jean Guenebault reported, on the testimony of Guilhermy himself, that the tracings had enabled the Baron to restore to all the tombs of Saint-Denis "leurs véritables épitaphes, singulièrement défigurées par l'un des architectes chargés de les rétablir après la destruction de l'important musée des Petits-Augustins où M. A. Lenoir les avait recueillis."[79] Guilhermy was exaggerating. Such work, as will be seen, lay in the future.

Gérente's mission did have the positive effect of furthering the interest of members of the Comité historique des arts et monuments in the Oxford drawings; it also provided fuller information regarding the drawings to such scholars as Michel Hennin, who was then compiling an inventory of the monuments of France.[80] Following Gérente's preliminary investigations, the Oxford drawings were viewed in the early summer of 1850 by Viollet-le-Duc and by two leading members of the Comité historique des arts et monuments, Léon de Laborde and Prosper Mérimée, Inspecteur général des monuments historiques et antiquités nationales. In Oxford Viollet-le-Duc became acquainted with John Henry Parker, the Oxford bookseller, publisher, and architectural historian, who was particularly interested in French Gothic buildings. He would later play a crucial role in securing for France tracings of all the Gaignières drawings in Oxford.[81]

---

[78] ADP, SSDB, kept with CA 1836–51 and Dossier 1841–76. Mesnages noted on 28 July 1848 that a number of the monuments were moved in connection with work in the crypt on the tenth-century remains of the church.

[79] Guenebault, "Notice," 47, especially n. 1.

[80] Guenebault, "Notice," n. 4, 46–47, for the use Hennin made of the Oxford collection in his *Dictionnaire iconographique.*

[81] *Bulletin du Comité historique des arts et monuments. Archéologie, Beaux-Arts* 2 (1850): 198–99; Pierre-Marie Auzas, *Eugène Viollet le Duc 1814–1879* (Paris: Caisse nationale des monuments historiques et des arts, 1979), 231 and also 76–79; Bruno Foucart et al., *Viollet-le-Duc. Galeries nationales du Grand Palais, 19 février-5 mai 1980* (Paris: Editions Réunion des Musées nationaux, Ministère de la Culture et de la Communication, 1980), 383. Viollet-le-Duc later drew on the Bodleian collection for his *Dictionnaire raisonné de l'architecture française du XIe au XVIe siècle,* 10 vols. (Paris: A. Morel, 1861–75), 9 (1875): 37, 44, 49, 51, 57, 61, 65, and his *Dictionnaire raisonné du mobilier français de l'époque carolingienne à la Renaissance,* 6 vols. (Paris: A. Morel, 1868–75), 2 (1871): 224–25, and, for his watercolor of the tomb of Philippe de Dreux (pl. 47), see Paul Prouté S. A., *Dessins originaux anciens et modernes* . . . (Catalogue périodique 84; Spring, 1985), 226, no. 220. He is more likely to have relied on the tracings of Gérente and Frappaz than to have prepared drawings when he was in Oxford. On the association of Laborde and Mérimée with the Comité, see Bercé, *Premiers travaux,* 5–6, 8–9. On Mérimée, see Pierre Trahard, *Prosper Mérimée de 1834 à 1853* (Bibliothèque Mérimée, 3; Paris: Honoré Champion, 1928), 145–47; and André Fermiger, "Mérimée et l'inspection des monuments historiques," in Nora et al., *La Nation,* 2: 593–611. On Laborde, see Jacques Henriet, in *Le "Gothique" retrouvé,* 71, no. 136; on Parker (1806–84), the notice by Warwick William Wroth, in *Dictionary of National Biography.* The Bodleian Library's Entry Books 8/1 and 8/2 (November 1844–June 1858, June 1858–December 1865) contain no indication that the Gaignières volumes were consulted during these years except by Jules Frappaz, who on 29 July 1861 used the volumes concerning Brie and Chartres, Beauvais, and Vendôme.

At the meeting of the Comité historique des arts et monuments held on 8 July 1850 (which Guilhermy attended), Laborde and Mérimée reported on their inspection of the Oxford drawings. As a letter of Mérimée suggests, their study had not been intensive.[82] In his report Laborde gave the number of volumes as fourteen and estimated that they contained some 3000 drawings.[83] However limited his knowledge of the collection, Laborde nonetheless enthusiastically acknowledged the importance of the drawings and recommended that tracings be made; he calculated that an artist, working at the rate of ten a day, could in six months reproduce the drawings of all the monuments which most closely concerned France's political and artistic history. The costs, he suggested, should be divided between the budget assigned to "Travaux historiques" and that of the Bibliothèque nationale. François Génin, the chief of the division, voiced his belief that the Bibliothèque nationale would in fact have to assume the entire burden of any such mission.[84]

Research continued. On 18 November 1850, after Génin reported to the Comité that the Oxford volumes had been stolen from France, the Comité discussed the possibility of recovering them. At this meeting Guilhermy first officially informed the Comité of Gérente's work. At the next meeting, on 9 December, he read Gérente's notes on the drawings and stressed the importance of the collection for the history, not only of Saint-Denis, but of the entire nation. At this meeting it was first suggested that, if the volumes could not be reacquired for France, their contents should be photographed.[85]

The Oxford drawings were considered at the Comité's following meeting, on 13 January 1851. Having discussed the Gaignières collection with conservators at the Bibliothèque nationale, Génin reported that the only inventory possessed by the Bibliothèque nationale was incomplete and vague, and that nothing was surely known regarding the provenance of the Oxford volumes. He still hoped that an exchange might be possible. Although he doubted that the Bibliothèque nationale would part with it, he suggested that the land survey of Ireland (which he described as "une sorte de Domesday-book relatif à l'Irlande") might suitably be offered. The

---

[82] Prosper Mérimée, *Lettres à une inconnue . . . ,* 2 vols. (Bibliothèque contemporaine; Paris: C. Lévy, 1873), 1: 309, a letter written at Salisbury on 15 June 1850.

[83] In 1847 (see above at n. 69) Viollet-le-Duc was aware of the actual number of volumes in the collection; Bouchot (*Inventaire,* xxvi) says that there were 1844 drawings at Oxford. In 1853 Guenebault reported that "cette partie de la collection se compose de treize, d'autres disent seize portefeuilles in-fo., lesquels renferment environ douze cents monuments funèbres": "Notice," 46; cf. 50, where, relying on the report of the Comité's *Bulletin,* he reported that there were almost 3000 drawings; see also ibid., 48, where, having consulted the inventory of the library of Gaignières prepared after his death, he observed that it then contained eighteen portfolios of drawings of funerary monuments. See n. 64 above.

[84] *Bulletin du Comité historique des arts et monuments. Archéologie, Beaux-Arts* 2 (1850): 198–99; see also the full account in Dauban, "Rapport," 165–81.

[85] "M. Génin annonce que les portefeuilles de Gaignières sont en Angleterre par suite d'un vol": *Bulletin du Comité historique des arts et monuments. Archéologie, Beaux-Arts* 2 (1850): 259; see also 3 (1852): 4.

Bibliothèque nationale, he said, could not afford to commission tracings of the Oxford drawings, but before the end of the year, money might become available from unused funds in the budget of the Missions scientifiques. He suggested that a plan of action be prepared. Laborde, who had waxed enthusiastic about the Oxford collection several months earlier, proposed that an expert be sent to Oxford to inventory the drawings and determine which should be copied. At the suggestion of Guilhermy, the Comité invited Viollet-le-Duc to give a detailed account of Gérente's findings. Viollet-le-Duc duly informed the Comité at its meeting on 10 March 1851 that he would be happy to present Gérente's catalogue and tracings; he was subsequently asked to display, in addition, photographs which Henri Le Secq had taken of various cathedrals.[86]

On 16 June 1851, Viollet-de-Duc submitted to the Comité "un grand nombre de dessins faisant partie de la collection Gaignières" at Oxford. Doubtless cognizant of the Comité's earlier discussions, Viollet-le-Duc suggested that, of the sixteen volumes of the Oxford collection, six merited being traced in their entirety. The contents of the rest, consisting primarily of epitaphs, could simply be copied. According to Viollet-le-Duc, Gérente's tracings—Guenebault believed they numbered two hundred[87]—were being exhibited in "une sorte de musée établi dans les magasins de Saint-Denis, et composé de débris d'architecture, de sculpture et de mosaïques recueillis à Saint-Denis, et qui n'ont pu trouver leur emploi dans les travaux de restauration." The Comité decided that Gérente's inventory of the Oxford drawings should be published in its *Bulletin*, and this was soon accomplished. Viollet-le-Duc next showed the Comité photographs which Le Secq had taken of the cathedrals of Reims, Amiens, Paris, and Chartres. Their "beauté" the Comité admired, and the wish to see thus recorded the most important monuments of the Middle Ages was expressed. No more, however, was said of photographing the Oxford drawings.[88]

---

[86] Ibid. 3 (1852): 34–35, 101. Nothing was said of the Oxford collection at the Comité's meetings of 10 February or 14 April 1851: ibid., 65, 129. On the two volumes of maps of Ireland (William Petty, *Down Survey of Ireland*) which were contemplated as a possible exchange for the Gaignières collection, see Delisle, *Cabinet des manuscrits,* 1: 333, and François Avril and Patricia Danz Stirnemann, *Manuscrits enluminés d'origine insulaire* (Paris: Bibliothèque nationale, 1987), no. 257. For the request of an Irish colonel to copy these volumes in 1786, see a letter of Le Noir, head of the library, dated 31 October 1786, which suggests that the English ambassador was also interested in them: Fernand Bournon, "Documents relatifs à la Bibliothèque du roi (1777–1791)," *La correspondance historique et archéologique* 15 (1908): 149–50.

[87] See above at n. 79.

[88] *Bulletin du Comité historique des arts et monuments. Archéologie, Beaux-Arts* 3 (1852): 194–95, 229–45, 269–88. On the work of Henri Le Secq (1818–82), see André Jammes and Eugenia Parry Janis, *The Art of French Calotype, with a Critical Dictionary of Photographers, 1834–1870* (Princeton: Princeton University Press, 1983), 206–10. For more detailed information on the photographs he took in 1850 and 1851, see Joel A. Herschman and William W. Clark, *Un voyage héliographique à faire. The Mission of 1851. The First Photographic Survey of Historical Monuments in France* (New York: Queens College, 1981), passim and especially 16–17. See also J. Grangedor, "Les derniers progrès de la photographie," *Gazette des Beaux-Arts,* 11e année, 2e pér., 1 (1869): 447–61, 533–42.

Louis-Jean Guenebault followed these developments closely, and with great interest. In 1853 he reported that all hope of recovering the Oxford drawings had been abandoned, but that an artist had been charged with continuing the work of Gérente and was even then working in Oxford, tracing all the drawings of monuments in the Gaignières collection.[89] Guenebault did not name this artist, nor did he give any details regarding his appointment, and it seems unlikely that, before 1860, any further steps were taken to obtain, in systematic fashion, copies of the Oxford drawings. Before then, however, Michel Hennin had become dissatisfied with Gérente's inventory, since he knew that the forty-eight pages published in the *Bulletin du Comité historique des arts et monuments* could not possibly record all the drawings in the collection, which he believed numbered some 3000. For his catalogue of artistic monuments relating to the history of France (which he was to publish in ten volumes between 1856 and 1863) he needed fuller information. Thus he contacted Bulkeley Bandinel, librarian of the Bodleian, and through him secured a far more complete listing, prepared by Alfred Hackman, a cataloguer at the Bodleian.[90] Later, in the 1860s, this inventory was used to record the progress which the artist Jules Frappaz would make in tracing the Oxford drawings.[91]

The publication of Gérente's catalogue awakened interest in the Oxford drawings among others who were not as centrally placed as Michel Hennin. In the spring of 1856 Stanislas Prioux, *correspondant* of the Ministère de l'Instruction publique at Lime near Braine, was sent to Oxford by the French government to determine the importance of the drawings for the history of his region. In the report he submitted on his return, he signaled thirty-two drawings of special interest, which concerned the abbeys of Saint-Yved of Braine and Longpont and the cathedrals of Soissons and Beauvais. During the ten days he spent in Oxford, he was assisted by both Hackmann and H. O. Coxe, then under-librarian at the Bodleian; he gathered information about the collection and traced the thirty-two drawings. Fourteen of them he used (six reproduced in handsome color) in the study

[89] Guenebault, "Notice," 47.

[90] Hennin, *Monuments,* 1: 269–81, 359; and Dauban, "Rapport," 170, n. 1. On Hackman (1811–74), who was appointed sub-librarian of the Bodleian in 1862, see W. A. Greenhill in *Dictionary of National Biography.* Under the date 22 November 1859 the Bodley Curators' Minutes for 1793–1862 record his work in cataloguing the Tanner manuscripts and the plans for his work on the new catalogue of the library; he was said to be receiving £150 (Bandinel's salary was £700) and to be "generally in the Library from 11:30 to 3 in the Winter and to 4 in the Summer."

[91] Hennin, who died on 29 December 1863, left his collection of documents and drawings relating to the history of France to the Bibliothèque nationale: Georges Duplessis, *Inventaire de la collection d'estampes relatives à l'histoire de France léguée en 1863 à la Bibliothèque nationale par M. Michel Hennin,* 5 vols. (Paris: Henri Menu, 1876–84), 5: ii–vi. See the copy of the catalogue which Hackman made for him, in BN, RE, Pe 1r, and particularly the note on the first page, which records that some items, traced by Frappaz, were not included in Hackman's inventory: see, e.g., 4–5, 23, 25. As Frappaz's tracings were received in Paris, they were ticked off against the listings in Hackman's catalogue.

of Saint-Yved of Braine which he published in 1859. Convinced that France was unlikely to obtain the volumes by exchange, Prioux strongly recommended that tracings of all the drawings be made; he estimated their number at 1500. On the basis of his own experience, he calculated that a year would suffice for the task. He suggested that, "pour remplir cette patriotique mission . . . et à peu de frais," each *département* should send a delegate charged with copying the drawings of particular interest to the region.[92]

This plan was never carried out, although a few drawings of monuments in Poitou and the Beauvaisis were made. The only concern for funerary monuments in the 1850s that the Bodleian's records reveal is that of a Mr. Pettigrew, whose request to use "Gough's Sepulchral Monuments" the Curators considered on 27 May 1854.[93] This situation altered, however, as the work of Viollet-le-Duc and Guilhermy at Saint-Denis progressed and as their plans to move the funerary monuments from the crypt to the upper church matured.

In 1867 Guilhermy wrote that Viollet-le-Duc had resolved some seven years earlier to restore the funerary monuments to the upper church. This decision, it seems clear, was made in 1859. By 1 May 1859 Viollet-le-Duc had prepared an elaborate plan illustrating—not with complete accuracy—the former disposition of some of the tombs of Saint-Denis and the areas in the crypt in which the eight coffins of the Bourbons might be placed, and where "des dispositions peuvent être prises pour la sépulture de la dynastie de Napoléon" (plate 16).[94] At the same time a serious campaign to acquire tracings of all the Oxford drawings commenced.

The first indication of such a project is found in a letter of 10 June 1859 which John Henry Parker (whom Viollet-le-Duc had seen in Oxford in 1850 and who in June 1858 had been made a corresponding associate of the Société des antiquaires de France) forwarded to the Curators of the Bodleian Library. He reported the French government's request to have "a set of facsimiles made of the entire collection of drawings framed by Mr. Gaignieres [sic] of tombs of the Princes and nobles of France now deposited in the Bodleian Library." According to Parker, he had been requested

---

[92] Prioux's report on his mission, authorized on 14 March 1856, was presented on 25 April 1856; it is printed in *Revue des Sociétés savantes des départements* 2 (1857): 60–62, as well as in the introduction to *Monographie de l'ancienne abbaye royale Saint-Yved de Braine avec la description des tombes royales et seigneuriales renfermés dans cette église* (Paris: Victor Didron, 1859), [1]–[3]. For the plates taken from the Oxford tracings ("Calqué à Oxford par S. Prioux"), see facing 42, 45, 59, 64, 70, 72, 84, 96 (in monochrome), and 54, 68, 74, 80, 82, 88 (in color).

[93] Dauban, "Rapport," 170, n. 1; Bodl., The Bodley Curators' Minutes (1793–1862). This Pettigrew may possibly be the surgeon and antiquarian, Thomas Joseph Pettigrew (1791–1865), treasurer of the British Archaeological Association; he abandoned surgery to dedicate himself to his antiquarian interests after his wife's death in 1854. See D'Arcy Power in *Dictionary of National Biography*.

[94] CRMH, Dessins Viollet-le-Duc, no. 8080 (MH 203696); see also no. 1194, dated 1 May 1859.

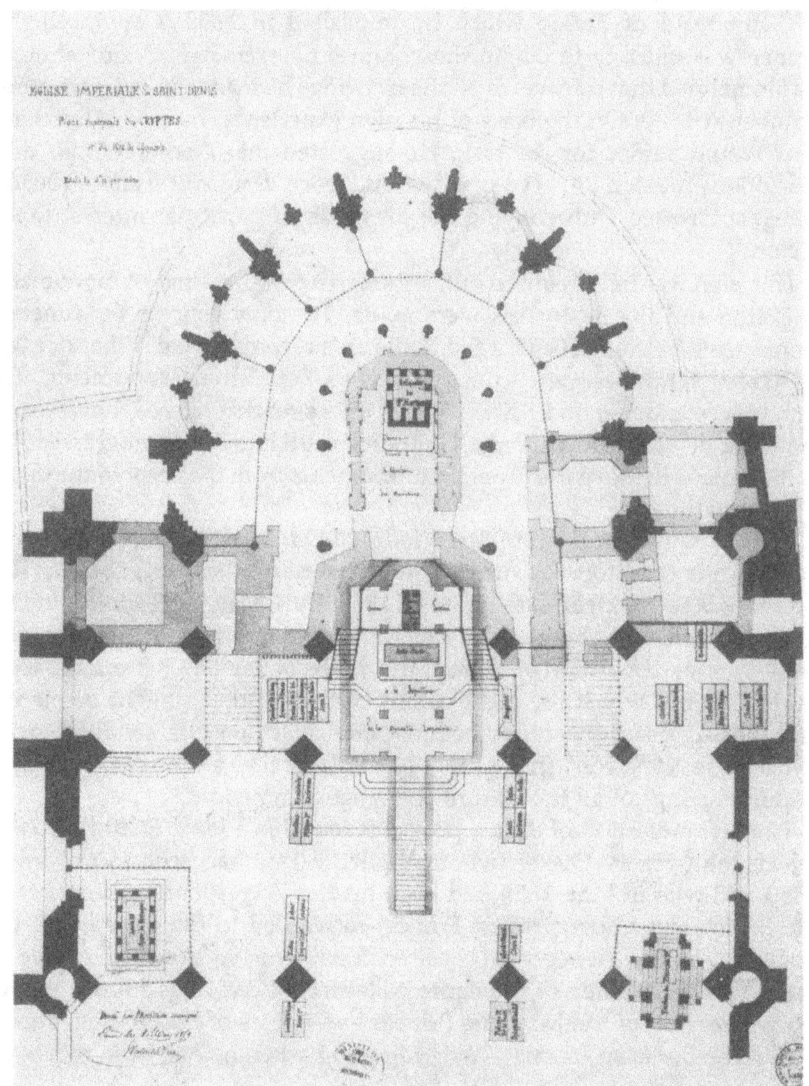

PLATE 16. Viollet-le-Duc, Plan of Saint-Denis (1 May 1859). Palais de Chaillot, Centre de recherche des monuments historiques, Dessins Viollet-le-Duc, no. 1194 (MH 203695). (Photographic Credit: Paris, Archives photographiques de la Direction du Patrimoine)

"to undertake it as a regular matter of business and to employ such artists" as he judged necessary.[95]

Prior debate in France had centered over whether the Oxford drawings should be photographed or traced. Despite the admiration the Comité historique des arts et monuments had shown in 1851 for the photographs

[95] Bodl., The Bodley Curators' Minutes (1793–1862). For Parker's election to the Société des antiquaires de France, see *Bulletin de la Société des antiquaires de France* (1858): 100–101.

of Le Secq, the advocates of the new process were in the end defeated, probably because of the costs involved. Those favoring photography noted that the reproductions would be more exact and that the project would be completed in just five or six months; colored drawings could be reproduced by having the photographs tinted. Their opponents stressed the risks involved. The durability of photographs had not been demonstrated; further, the process was expensive, since photographing 3000 drawings (the number still believed to exist in Oxford) would cost between 30,000 and 36,000 francs. Parker had estimated that in England the cost of tracing what he believed amounted to 1952 drawings would be more than 25,000 francs, but the day was definitively carried in favor of tracings when Jules Frappaz, an artist known to the Comité because of work he had done in 1853–54, offered to copy 3,000 drawings for 10,000 francs. Frappaz's proposal was eminently attractive, but the Comité decided that, although there was need for haste, Frappaz should not be exploited. His bid had been made in the absence of close familiarity with the drawings and first-hand knowledge of the task. Therefore he should first be sent to Oxford to evaluate the situation and submit some drawings to the Comité; if he then wished to withdraw, the Comité would have at least something to show for his labors. There was little delay. By the end of February 1860 Frappaz had received a commission. He was given 16,000 francs for two years' work, and it was reported that the drawings he had already submitted were excellent.[96]

Frappaz's formal introduction to Oxford as the delegate of the French government took place on 16 June 1860. On that date the Ministre de l'Instruction publique et des Cultes wrote the vice-chancellor of Oxford to inform him that Frappaz, described as "Peintre dessinateur," had been charged with making copies of the Oxford drawings. Access to them and all possible assistance were requested. In addition the Ministre asked, "par un motif que vous apprécierez," that each of Frappaz's tracings be collated with the original and be given the approval of the Bodleian Library.[97]

The drawings which Frappaz dated indicate that he worked in Oxford between 1860 and 1863, and that the bulk of his work was completed in 1860 and 1861.[98] His drawings were approved by Bandinel, who resigned

---

[96] Dauban, "Rapport," 178–81, and see particularly 178, n. 2 on the confusion regarding the number of drawings in Oxford which were to be traced, which Dauban hypothesized had arisen because in some cases several drawings were catalogued together. For Frappaz's earlier work for the Comité, see Bercé, *Premiers travaux,* 335–36.

[97] Bodl., L. P. Correspondence, 1a/2, fol. 229. The Bodleian Library was extremely cooperative with requests of the French government which were presented at this time. On 3 June 1865 permission was given for the loan of various manuscripts to the Imprimerie nationale for two months: Bodl., The Bodley Curators' Meetings (1854–1868), Registrar's Notes, fol. 139.

[98] Duplessis, "Gaignières," 486. For 1862, see Paris, BN, RE, Pe 1, fol. 10; for 1863, Pe 1, fol. 22. Maddan, *Summary Catalogue,* 4: 295, suggests that he worked between 1860 and 1866, whereas Macray indicates that he had finished in 1860: Macray, *Annals of the Bodleian Library,* 285–89.

his post as librarian in 1860 but apparently continued, as honorary curator, to validate Frappaz's work in the few weeks of 1861 before his death on 6 February.[99] H. O. Coxe, who succeeded Bandinel as librarian on 6 November 1860, also approved Frappaz's drawings, both as under-librarian, before his promotion, and afterwards, as librarian.[100] Only a few of the drawings were sent back to France without validation.[101] The titles possessed by Bandinel and Coxe when they approved Frappaz's copies and the dates which Frappaz affixed to many of them show that he did not proceed entirely systematically. Rather, at least at the beginning, he skipped from volume to volume, perhaps to demonstrate to the Comité the range of monuments and objects recorded in the collection.[102]

Frappaz's tracings are extremely faithful (cf. plates 17 and 18), even if he occasionally neglected to reproduce the pencil underdrawing, notes, and touches of color found on the originals.[103] In one instance Frappaz did not recopy a piece of which two reproductions appear in the original volume,[104] although in another case a duplicate was traced.[105] Occasionally

[99] Richard Garnett, in *Dictionary of National Biography*. For validations by Bandinel in 1861, see BN, RE, Pe 1, fols. 99, 100; Pe 1a, fol. 26; Pe 1p, fols. 67, 69. The accuracy of Frappaz's dating is questionable, since a drawing initialed by him and dated 1861 was approved by Coxe as under-librarian, although he had become librarian in November 1860.

[100] Craster, *History of the Bodleian Library*, 43.

[101] See, e.g., BN, RE, Pe 1, fols. 5–6, 8, 78–79; Pe 1g, fol. 233; Pe Im, fols. 60, 61.

[102] The first volume (BN, RE, Pe 1; BL, GD-G 1) contains validations by both Coxe (acting as both under-librarian and librarian) and Bandinel; most of the tracings were executed in 1861, although the one on fol. 76 was done in 1860, and that on fol. 10 in 1862. The volume relating to the Ile-de-France, which was catalogued as the third volume when Frappaz was working in Oxford (BN, RE, Pe 1b; Bodl., GD-G 12), appears to have been traced early in Frappaz's stay. All the tracings in this volume were validated by Bandinel, and the complex validation formulas employed on fols. 77–86 suggest that, when they were approved, Bandinel was paying particularly close attention to his task; the drawings in the volume that are dated were completed in 1860. The last volume (BN, RE, Pe 1p; Bodl., GD-G 16) contains tracings executed in both 1860 and 1861; they were validated by both Bandinel and Coxe, each acting as librarian. The second volume of the series devoted to Paris, catalogued as the tenth volume of the collection when Frappaz was in Oxford (BN, RE, Pe 1j; Bodl., GD-G 4) contains many validations by Coxe, acting as under-librarian; Bandinel approved a substantial number of the tracings. The volume that was catalogued as the eleventh volume of the collection in the 1860s (BN, RE, Pe 1k; Bodl., GD-G 5) was traced in 1861; all tracings were validated by Coxe as librarian. This is also true of the volume then catalogued as the twelfth volume of the collection (BN, RE, Pe 1l; Bodl., GD-G 6); Coxe likewise validated as librarian all the drawings in what was then the fourth volume of the collection (BN, RE, Pe 1c; Bodl., GD-G 7).

[103] See, e.g., BN, RE, Pe 1 (Bodl., GD-G 1), fols. 8, 68, 101; BN, RE, Pe 1a (Bodl., GD-G 2), fols. 2, 42; BN, RE, Pe 1h (Bodl., GD-G 15), fol. 148; BN, RE, Pe 1k (Bodl., GD-G 5), fols. 17, 19; BN, RE, Pe 1o (Bodl., GD-G 10), fols. 1b, 44, 66–86. The original color drawing of a now-lost beaker suggests, through careful cutting of the paper, the three-dimensionality of the cup; this aspect of the original is not reproduced in Frappaz's otherwise faithful duplicate: BN, RE, Pe 1p (Bodl., GD-G 16), fol. 63; see Bonnie Young, "The Monkey and the Peddlar," *Metropolitan Museum of Art Bulletin* (June 1968): pl. 13, p. 451, a photograph of the original drawing.

[104] BN, RE, Pe 1 (Bodl., GD-G 1), fols. 10–11; in the Paris volume, fol. 10, a penciled note indicates that "Le folio 11 de la Collection d'Oxford n'offre que la répétition de cette pièce"; the Paris volume contains no fol. 11.

[105] BN, RE, Pe 1d (Bodl., GD-G 8), fols. 42–43.

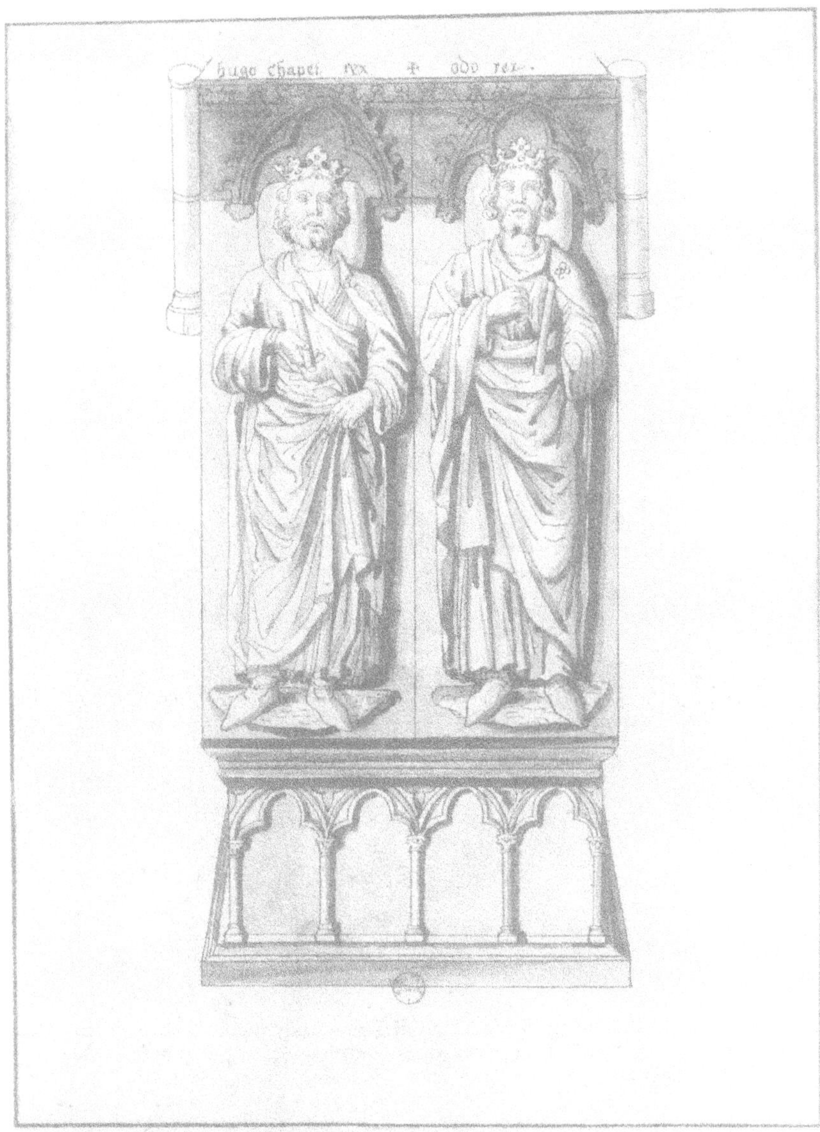

PLATE 17. Frappaz Tracing of the Gaignières Drawing of the Tomb of Eudes and Hugues Capet at Saint-Denis. Paris, Bibliothèque nationale, Réserve des estampes, Pe 1a, fol. 15. (Photographic Credit: Paris, Bibliothèque nationale)

epitaphs which were begun on the face and continued on the reverse of the Gaignières drawings were completed on the faces of Frappaz's copies, and, although the epitaphs are carefully reproduced, there are discrepancies in

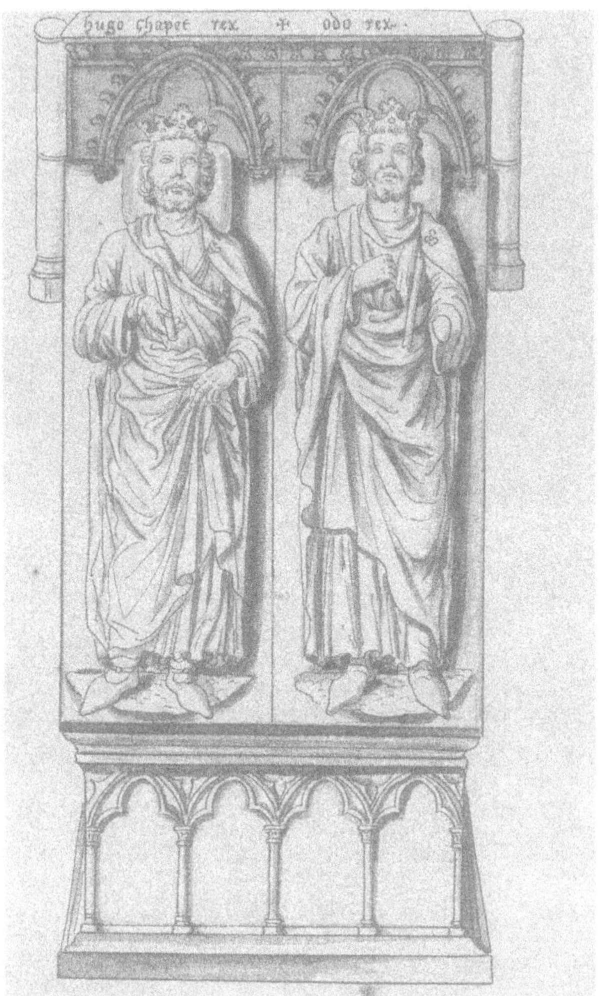

PLATE 18. Gaignières Drawing of the Tomb of Eudes and Hugues Capet at Saint-Denis. Oxford, Bodleian Library, MS. Gough Drawings-Gaignières II, fol. 15. (Photographic Credit: Oxford, Bodleian Library)

punctuation and accenting.[106] Frappaz did not indicate the original drawings that had been executed on parchment rather than on paper, nor did he note which drawings had been cut out after execution for subsequent mounting.[107] The tracings are nonetheless entirely adequate copies of the original drawings. On 18 July 1890 the Conservateur of the Musée archéologique of Nantes wrote to the Bodleian Library questioning the

[106] BN, RE, Pe 1 (Bodl., GD-G 1), fols. 8, 56, 65–66, 75, 78; BN, RE, Pe 1c (Bodl., GD-G 7), fol. 124.

[107] See, for example, BN, RE, Pe 1a (Bodl., GD-G 2), fols. 4, 24–25, 31.

faithfulness of Frappaz's reproduction of the tomb of Arthur III, duke of Brittany, but his suspicions proved unfounded.[108]

By October 1860 Frappaz's work had attracted admiring attention in England.[109] The tracings were sent periodically to France where, on arrival, they were checked off against the copy of the inventory which Hackman had prepared for Hennin.[110] Their presence in France stimulated renewed interest in the Oxford originals, and in 1862 Edgard Boutaric reported that a series of judicial documents in the Archives impériales showed that the drawings had been stolen from the Bibliothèque royale between 1781 and 1784.[111] The availability of the tracings in Paris, however, was not well publicized. On 24 January 1868, the mayor of Le Bignon (near Nantes), apparently unaware that tracings existed in France, wrote to the Bodleian Library to request a list of the drawings of tombs—at least of those relating to the Maine—to be found in the Gaignières collection, and to ask for an estimate of the cost of copies.[112]

In April 1862 Guilhermy and Viollet-le-Duc were putting the drawings to good use as they shifted tombs from the crypt of Saint-Denis to the upper church. As early as April 1860, restoration of Dagobert's monument—split in half by Debret—had begun.[113] Guilhermy knew Montfaucon's volumes, as well as the various catalogues of Lenoir; he was also familiar with the works of Doublet, Millet, and Félibien.[114] Thus, like his predecessors, he could have identified with little difficulty the monuments at Saint-Denis. Nonetheless, because "les noms avaient été intervertis, par suite des divers déplacements de ces figures," he believed it essential "les revoir avec les Dessins de Gaignières, dont les copies, faites à Oxford, sont déposés à la Bibliothèque royale [sic]."[115]

---

[108] BN, RE, Pe 1 (Bodl., GD-G 1), fol. 103b/104; the letter is found in the Oxford volume, facing this folio.

[109] Gagliani, in *The Gentleman's Magazine* 209 (October 1860), 406, who refers to the "Rapport" of Dauban; like so many others, Gagliani was confused regarding the number of drawings at Oxford, which he gave as 3000.

[110] BN, RE, Pe 1r, fol. A.

[111] See Appendix III below. A note to the communication reported that some copies had been received at the Ministère de l'Instruction publique: *Bulletin de la Société impériale des antiquaires de France* (1862): 86, n. 1.

[112] The Mayor, A. Juays des Touches, suggested that on "folios 200–205–219" might be found drawings of monuments such as those he was seeking: Bodl., LP Correspondence 3/1, fol. 96. In fact, two volumes of the Oxford collection (BN, RE, Pe 1f–1g, 1h; Bodl., GD-G 14–15) contain drawings relating to the Maine, and in the second of these volumes a number of drawings of monuments of that region appear between fols. 200 and 219.

[113] Guilhermy, BN, n.a.f. 6122, fol. 143; see ibid., fol. 145v for 1862–63, when, Guilhermy noted, "Il s'agit maintenant de peindre le monument"; and ibid., fols. 147, 149v, and 151 for work on the monument in 1864 and 1865. For Debret's installation of the monument in 1817, see AN, F^{21} 1451, Debret, fol. 24; for his work on the monument in 1843, see AN, F^{13} 528A, Dossier "Compte rendu des Travaux exécutés en 1843." See also Bideault, "Tombeau de Dagobert," 28–29; and Viollet-le-Duc, *Dictionnaire . . . architecture*, 9: 34, n. 2.

[114] See, e.g., Guilhermy, BN, n.a.f. 6121, fols. 130, 150, 157–60v, 164, 192v, for his use of Montfaucon; ibid., fols. 159v–60, for Lenoir; ibid., fols. 105–7v, 115–16, 226, for Doublet; ibid., fols. 106v, 108, 116, 121, 150, 227, 283, for Millet; ibid., fol. 240, for Félibien.

[115] Guilhermy, BN, n.a.f. 6122, fol. 145v; and Viollet-le-Duc, *Dictionnaire . . . architecture*, 9: 47, n. 2.

In April 1862 thirteen monuments were removed from the crypt to the upper church. Apparently at this time or shortly afterwards Guilhermy became aware that the two missing effigies of the 1260s were those of Eudes and Hugues Capet. Noting that, in the absence of their cenotaph, there would be more room than otherwise at the entry to the choir on the north side of the crossing, he considered having incised on two stones the names "des deux princes privés de leurs effigies." This, however, was never done, perhaps because Guilhermy recalled the harsh criticism which Debret's inscriptions had aroused. At the same time, Guilhermy realized that in 1848 he had incorrectly identified four of the effigies carved in the 1260s.[116]

Work on the tombs progressed during the fall of 1864. By mid-November no more than five or six monuments remained in the crypt; by 17 April 1865 tombs had been arranged in the chapel of Saint-Hippolyte and in the crossing. Guilhermy was still concerned with the correct identities of the gisants of the 1260s. In October 1866 he again compared them with Frappaz's tracings of the Oxford drawings by making extensive notes from the drawings for verification at Saint-Denis.[117]

In 1867 the installation of the tombs in the upper church had apparently been completed (plate 19).[118] In the book he published that year, Guilhermy acknowledged that it was thanks to the "portefeuilles de la collection de Gaignières qu'on a pu rendre à chacune son véritable nom." He said that, if one day he should rewrite his *Monographie* of 1848 on Saint-Denis, he would rectify the errors which had been made, for which, however, he denied responsibility.[119] Neither he nor Viollet-le-Duc actually saw to the obliteration of all the inscriptions which Debret had had incised on the tombs. This Guilhermy had claimed was essential in his *Monographie*, a judgment he forcefully repeated in 1862–63, when he asserted that it was in fact being accomplished.[120] The new cenotaphs which Viollet-le-

[116] Ibid.; see also the book on Saint-Denis which he published with Charles Fichot in 1867, *Eglise impériale*, 46.

[117] Guilhermy, BN, n.a.f. 6122, fols. 147–50, 153–55v.

[118] Jules Jaquemet, *L'église de Saint-Denis, sa crypte, ses tombeaux, ses chapelles, son trésor* (Paris: Putois-Crette, 1867), 41; L'abbé Testory, *L'église de Saint-Denis et ses tombeaux royales* (Paris: De Rochette, 1870), 66; Guilhermy and Fichot, *Eglise impériale*, 26–55, especially 32. See also Guilhermy, BN, n.a.f. 6122, fol. 156 for later repairs of the funerary monuments, in part occasioned by the events of 1870. On the restoration of the tombs, said to have been executed "sans plan méthodique," see Paul Vitry and Gaston Brière, *L'église abbatiale de Saint-Denis et ses tombeaux. Notice historique et archéologique*, 2nd ed. (Paris: Henri Laurens, 1948), 31; for other criticisms, see the letter of Viollet-le-Duc, printed on 19 January 1877 in *Le Figaro*, in Guilhermy, BN, n.a.f. 6122, pièce 2.

[119] "Si nous avions à refaire un jour la monographie de Saint-Denis, nous ne manquerions pas d'y rectifier des erreurs dont la responsabilité ne doit pas être à notre charge": Guilhermy and Fichot, *Eglise impériale*, 46. Correct identifications were inserted in the various editions of Guilhermy's work on Saint-Denis, published in 1867 and later years; the drawing originally identified as Carloman I appears as Clovis II, those originally said to represent Robert and Clovis III are designated Clovis III and Carloman II. See above, 30–31.

[120] "Il faudra donc gratter la pierre, à mesure qu'on découvrira les erreurs commises dans le classement": Guilhermy, *Monographie*, 215. In 1862–63 he noted, "A mesure que les effigies reprennent leurs véritables noms, on fait disparaître ceux qui avaient été gravées sur les dalles par ordre de M. Debret": Guilhermy, BN, n.a.f. 6122, fol. 145v.

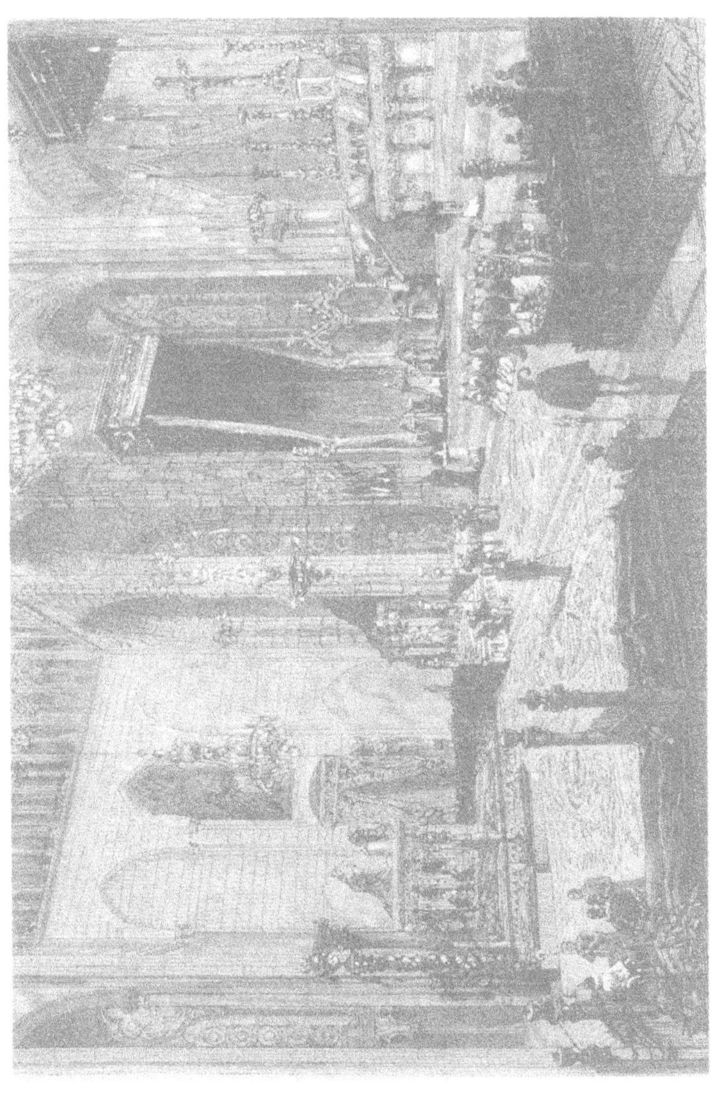

PLATE 19. Consecration of the Basilique de Saint-Denis after its Restoration, Sunday, 11 October [1868]. Paris, Bibliothèque Nationale, Cabinet des estampes, 77 B 74825. (Photographic Credit: Paris, Bibliothèque nationale)

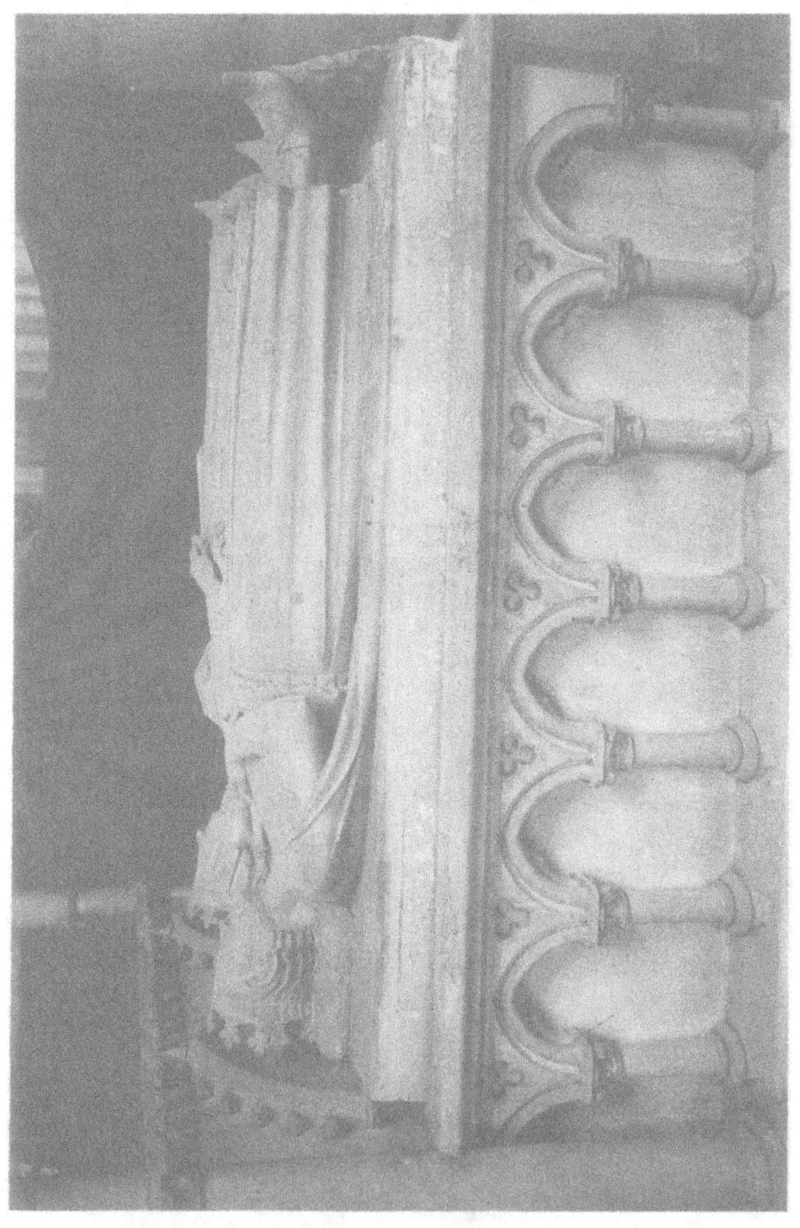

PLATE 20. The Tomb of Carloman I and Hermentrude, 1956. Archives de la Direction du Patrimoine, Seine-Saint-Denis, Basilique, no. 1238, Travaux 6°, 1953 à 1958 (Devis no. 535/1956 [1 juin 1956]) (MH 86. 868). (Photographic Credit: Paris, Archives photographiques de la Direction du Patrimoine)

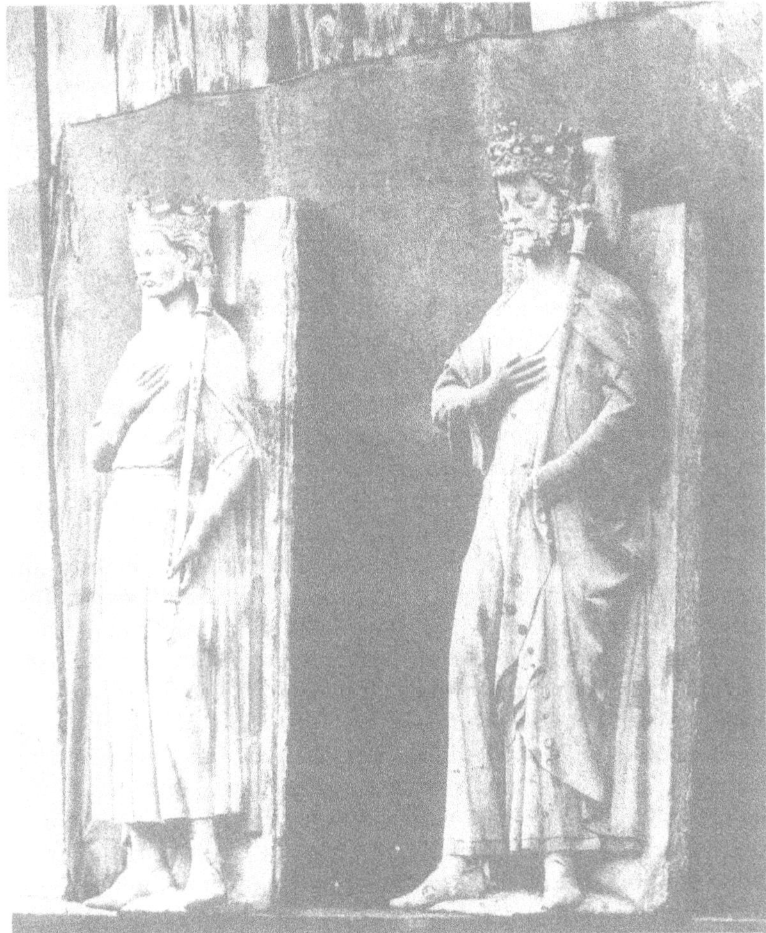

PLATE 21. Effigies of Carloman I and Robert the Pious. Fichot, "Tombeaux," Paris, Bibliothèque nationale, Cabinet des estampes, Pe 12a, no. 21 (B 14919). (Photographic Credit: Bibliothèque nationale)

Duc designed and had executed for the tombs meant that at least the inscriptions on the bases of the monuments disappeared forever (plate 20).

Apparently as they were being transferred from the crypt to the upper church, and before their final installations on Viollet-le-Duc's elaborate bases, the monuments were carefully photographed, and in 1867 Charles Fichot (who had done the engravings for Guilhermy's *Monographie* in 1848 and had worked with him on the book on Saint-Denis that appeared in 1867) published two volumes of these photographs (plate 21).[121] Thus, in

---

[121] BN, Cabinet des estampes, Pe 12a–b, "Tombeaux et figures historiques de l'Eglise Imperiale de Saint-Denis." I am grateful to Nancy Rash for bringing these volumes to my attention. I have been unable to discover any additional copies of these volumes or the whereabouts of the negatives.

the end, photography was enlisted in the service of the tombs of Saint-Denis, even if that new and risky process had, less than twenty years before, been rejected as a means of acquiring for France copies of the Gaignières drawings in Oxford.

The effort expended by Viollet-le-Duc and Guilhermy to restore the tombs of Saint-Denis to their medieval splendor was undone in the 1950s, when the monuments were dismounted from their imposing nineteenth-century cenotaphs and mounted on simple blocks of stone.[122] The identifications of the tombs which Guilhermy so laboriously effected in the 1860s have nonetheless proved remarkably accurate, although a number of the effigies at Saint-Denis still bear the erroneous inscriptions with which they were incised between 1839 and 1841. In addition, Frappaz's tracings still serve as useful supplements to the original drawings of the Gaignières collection in the Bibliothèque nationale, although, owing to the quality of the paper on which they were executed, many of them have withstood the passage of time less well than the identifications of the tombs which they facilitated.[123]

The use made of the Oxford collection of Gaignières drawings in the mid-nineteenth century brought them to the attention of scholars in Europe and, eventually, America. It is a tribute to the continuing utility of these drawings, as well as to the faith which some in the early 1850s placed in the future of photography, that in the 1960s—a hundred years after Frappaz copied them at Oxford, two centuries and a half after they were made—a complete collection of photographs of the Gaignières drawings at Oxford and of the companion volumes of drawings of funerary monuments at the Bibliothèque nationale was acquired and inventoried in New York City, for Columbia University.[124] There, in Paris, and in Oxford the drawings continue to provide access—in many cases the only access—to the monuments which Roger de Gaignières aimed to advance when, with his secretary and artist, Barthélemy Remy and Louis Boudan, he traveled throughout France, recording the memorials of his country's past.

---

[122] Brown, "Burying and Unburying," 259.

[123] See, e.g., BN, RE, Pe 1c (Bodl., GD-G 7), fols. 26, 41, 129; BN, RE, Pe 1d (Bodl., GD-G 8), fols. 99, 131, 135.

[124] The collection at Columbia, housed in the Photograph Collection of the Department of Art History and Archaeology (the Vogel Study Room), was established by Robert Branner, who on 12 March 1964 ordered from the Bibliothèque nationale photographs of the drawings in volumes Pe 2-Pe 11c of the Réserve des estampes, and who in August 1965 arranged, with the cooperation of the Bodleian Library, to have prints made from the negative microfilms of the sixteen volumes of the Oxford collection which the Metropolitan Museum of Art possessed; this collection of prints supplements that of some hundred photographs of the tombs of Saint-Denis which Branner acquired for Columbia in 1963–64. At Columbia the microfilms of the Bibliothèque nationale volumes, as well as mounted photographs of all the drawings in these volumes and of those in the Oxford collection, are available for study. I am indebted to Shirley Branner, Kathryn Kramer, Patricia Danz Stirnemann, Georgia Sommers Wright, and, most particularly, Helene Farrow for information regarding the Columbia collection, and to Mary Doherty, Jane Hayward, and Charles Little for assistance concerning the collection at the Metropolitan Museum. Michael Evans has kindly informed me that the Courtauld Institute in London also possesses an extensive, although apparently incomplete, set of photographs of the Gaignières drawings of funerary monuments.

APPENDIX I

THE OXFORD COLLECTION OF GAIGNIERES DRAWINGS AND THE TRACINGS OF THE BIBLIOTHEQUE NATIONALE

A Concordance

Title of Volume	*Volume Numbers Assigned by*			
	Viollet-le-Duc	Gérente and Hennin	B.N.	Oxford
Tombeaux des princes du sang royal	I	I	Pe 1	1 (18346)
Tombeaux des Rois et Reines de France	II	II	Pe 1a	2 (18347)
Tombeaux et épitaphes des églises de l'Ile de France	IX	III	Pe 1b	12 (18357)
Tombeaux et épitaphes des églises de Normandie, tome I	VII	IV	Pe 1c	7 (18352)
Tombeaux et épitaphes des églises de Normandie, tome II	VIII	V	Pe 1d	8 (18353)
Tombeaux et épitaphes des églises de Valois et Bissonne	X	VI	Pe 1e	13 (18358) ("VI" inside cover)
Tombeaux et épitaphes des églises de France (d'Angers, de Nantes, de Loches, de Tours, du Mans), tome I	XIV (unbound)	VII	Pe 1f Pe 1g	14 (18359)
Tombeaux et épitaphes des églises de France, tome II	XV (unbound)	VIII	Pe 1h	15 (18360)
Tombeaux et épitaphes des églises de Paris, tome I	III	IX	Pe 1i	3 (18348)
Tombeaux et épitaphes des églises de Paris, tome II	IV	X	Pe 1j	4 (18349)
Tombeaux et épitaphes des églises de Paris, tome III	V	XI	Pe 1k	5 (18350)
Tombeaux et épitaphes des églises de Paris, tome IV	VI	XII	Pe 1l	6 (18351)

APPENDIX I—*Continued*

THE OXFORD COLLECTION OF GAIGNIERES DRAWINGS AND THE TRACINGS OF THE BIBLIOTHEQUE NATIONALE

A Concordance

Title of Volume	*Volume Numbers Assigned by*			
	Viollet-le-Duc	Gérente and Hennin	B.N.	Oxford
Tombeaux et épitaphes des églises de France. Champagne et Bourgogne.	XI	XIII	Pe 1m	11 (18356) ("XIII" inside cover)
Tombeaux et épitaphes des églises de France. Beauvais, Chartres, Vendôme.	XII	XIV	Pe 1n	9 (18354) ("14" inside cover)
Tombeaux et épitaphes des églises de France. Brie.	XIII	XV	Pe 1o	10 (18355) ("XV" inside cover)
Recueil d'armes et de devises tirées sur plusieurs anciens monuments, vitres, bastimens, tableaux, tapisseries, manuscrits originaux, etc.	XVI	XVI	Pe 1p	16 (18361)

For the listing of volumes by Viollet-le Duc, see ADP, SSDB, Dossier 1841–76, fol. 130v.

For the listing of volumes by Gérente, see *Bulletin du Comité historique des arts et monuments. Archéologie, Beaux-Arts* 3 (1852): 229.

For the similar listing of volumes in the catalogue prepared for Hennin, see BN, RE, Pe 1r.

The designations of the volumes in BN, RE, and in Bodl. are those in use today. For the Bibliothèque nationale, see Bouchot, *Inventaire,* 1: nos. 1849–3792. For the Bodleian, see Madan, *Summary Catalogue,* 4: 295–96.

APPENDIX II

THOMAS KERRICH'S DRAWINGS AND ENGRAVINGS OF FRENCH MONUMENTS

Thomas Kerrich (1748–1838), for twenty-one years librarian of Cambridge, was a talented draftsman and engraver,[125] as dedicated as Montfaucon, Gaignières, and his fellow-countrymen Richard Gough and Charles Alfred Stothard (1786–1821) to recording memorials of the Middle Ages. However, his travels in Belgium, Germany, Italy, and France between 1771 and 1774 gave him a perspective that was broader than theirs. Among his papers are preserved drawings and richly annotated sketches made during his visits to these European countries, as well as numerous drawings made in England.[126] Among them are many funerary effigies; his drawings inspired Stothard to publish his own collection of depictions of tombs, and Kerrich himself contributed a number of illustrations to Richard Gough's *English Sepulchral Monuments.*[127] Kerrich was also interested in the history of architecture, and two of his four published papers dealt perceptively with Gothic structures.[128] Particularly attracted by Italian monuments, he nonetheless acknowledged the excellence of French medieval sculpture and architecture and observed that if the

---

[125] The best available sources for the life and work of Thomas Kerrich are the articles by Thompson Cooper in *Dictionary of National Biography,* and Nichols, *Illustrations,* 6: 807–29; see 814 for a list of Kerrich's engravings known to Nichols. Pamela Tudor-Craig is currently preparing a full study of Kerrich.

[126] BL, Add. Mss. 6728–76, a collection bequeathed to the British Museum on Kerrich's death, which includes the papers of the Cambridge architect, James Essex (1722–84), in volumes 6760–73 and 6776. On Essex and his relations with Kerrich, see the catalogue of the bicentenary exhibition in Essex's honor: Thomas Cocke, *The Ingenious Mr. Essex, Architect* (Cambridge: Fitzwilliam Museum, 1984). For Kerrich's will, drawn on 2 March 1827 and proved on 5 June 1828, see London, Public Record Office, Prob 11/1742, and the Prerogative Court of Canterbury, 366 Sutton. I consulted a copy of the will at the Society of Antiquaries in London.

[127] Nichols, *Illustrations,* 6: 812–14. For Gough, see above, at n. 7. Preparatory drawings for some of the illustrations which Kerrich furnished to Gough are found in BL, Add. Ms. 6730, especially fols. 33–34, 42, 46–48, 50–53, 64–65. On Stothard, see the article by Edward Irving Carlyle in *Dictionary of National Biography* and Stothard's own work (with Alfred John Kempe), *The Monumental Effigies of Great Britain, Selected from our Cathedrals and Chapters, for the Purpose of Bringing Together, and Preserving Representations of the Best Historical Illustrations Extant, from the Norman Conquest to the Reign of Henry the Eighth,* 2 vols. (London: J. M'Creery, [1811]–1817).

[128] Thomas Kerrich, "Some Observations on the Gothic Buildings Abroad, Particularly Those of Italy, and on Gothic Architecture in General," *Archaeologia* 16 (1812): 292–325; idem, "Observations on the Use of the Mysterious Figure, Called Vesica Piscis, in the Architecture of the Middle Ages, and in Gothic Architecture," *Archaeologia* 19 (1821): 353–68.

French monuments "were the work of native Frenchmen, we may justly entertain great doubts whether Italy did really take the lead in the arts as soon as has been generally believed."[129]

Because of the destruction which the Revolution visited on France, the drawings and notes Kerrich made in Paris, where he stayed for six months, are important, particularly since he concentrated not on the well-documented tombs of Saint-Denis but rather on those of other churches. Kerrich did visit Saint-Denis, where he was especially impressed by the tomb of Charles the Bald, and where he drew the tomb of Bertrand du Guesclin; as a record of royal monuments there, however, he relied on the engravings of Jean Rabel published in Pierre Bonfons's guide to Paris of 1605.[130] At Notre-Dame Kerrich did four sketches of the tomb of Jean Juvenal des Ursins and took notes on the monument of Guillaume Juvenal des Ursins; more important, he made six heavily annotated drawings of the equestrian statue of Philip IV, which he identified correctly but finally concluded, on the authority of Corrozet's guide to Paris, was a representation of Philip VI.[131]

Kerrich's major and most systematic efforts in Paris were concentrated on the churches of the Cordeliers and of the Jacobins of the Rue Saint-Jacques. He made several drawings of two funerary monuments at the Cordeliers and of nine from the Jacobins. He was, understandably, surer of the identities of the effigies at the Jacobins than of those at the Cordeliers, where the fire of 1580 had obliterated inscriptions.[132]

Of the two monuments he drew at the Cordeliers, one was a gisant bearing the arms of France surmounted by a label of four points. This effigy, as has been seen, had been and would later be said to be that of Philip V as count of Poitiers and, alternatively, Pierre of Alençon, before being identified in 1879 as the tomb of Robert l'Enfant of Artois.[133] When Kerrich saw it, it was designated as Charles of Etampes, but because of the arms on the buckler (which Kerrich did not draw), Kerrich mistrusted this identification. He made five sketches of the effigy and eventually decided that it must represent Louis, son of Charles of Valois and count of Alençon

---

[129] Thomas Kerrich, "Observations upon Some Sepulchral Monuments in Italy and France," *Archaeologia* 18 (1815–17): 193–94.

[130] Ibid., 188; BL, Add. Ms. 6728, fol. 175; see Add. Ms. 6729, fols. 124–25 for plates cut from the 1605 edition of Bonfons's work, *Les Fastes, Antiqvitez et choses plvs remarqvables de Paris. Labeur de curieuse et diligente recherche, divisé en quatre livres* (Paris: Nicolas and Pierre Bonfons, 1605), fols. 61, 65, 69, 73; on this book and its source, the guide of Corrozet, see Dumolin, "Notes sur les vieux guides de Paris," 209–33. For a drawing of a statue at the Sainte-Chapelle, see BL, Add. Ms. 6728, fol. 86; for drawings executed in Dijon, Saint-Omer, and Cambrai, ibid., fols. 167v–68, 197v–98, 202–3.

[131] BL, Add. Ms. 6728, fols. 124–26, 204–5, 216; see Françoise Baron, "Le cavalier royal de Notre-Dame de Paris et le problème de la statue équestre au moyen âge," *Bulletin monumental* 126 (1968): 141–54, who does not mention Kerrich's sketches. His drawings of the monument were executed sometime after the spring of 1773: BL, Add. Ms. 6728, fol. 125; see also fol. 124v.

[132] See n. 21 above. For a detailed listing of the sketches and of the engravings which Kerrich later made, see Table A.

[133] See above, following n. 21.

(d. 1328), whose arms were, like those of Pierre of Alençon, *semé de France à la bordure de gueules.*[134]

The other monument at the Cordeliers, of which Kerrich made four sketches, was apparently unidentified at the church. Kerrich, however, correctly surmised that it was the gisant of Charles, count of Etampes (d. 1336).[135] Kerrich may have used two Gaignières drawings of this gisant to make his identification; other sketches he executed were based on drawings "in the King's Cabinet, Paris," which suggests that he had access to the royal collection.[136] On the other hand, he may have deduced the gisant's identity simply from the arms on the buckler (*semé de France, au bâton componné d'hermines et de gueules*) and from information in Anselme, Corrozet, or Bonfons.[137]

With the monuments at the Jacobins Kerrich had far less difficulty. He executed and correctly identified three drawings of the heart tomb of Charles, count of Anjou and king of Naples (d. 1285); seven of the gisant of Philip of Artois, lord of Conches (d. 1298); five of the effigy of Robert, count of Clermont (d. 1318); three of the monument of Louis of Evreux (d. 1319); three of that of Charles of Valois (d. 1325); six of the gisant of Louis, count of Clermont (d. 1342); four of that of Charles of Valois, count of Alençon (d. 1346); one of the entrail tomb of Philip VI (d. 1350); and five of the monument of Pierre, duke of Bourbon and count of Clermont and La Marche (d. 1356).[138]

Kerrich was not completely sure of the identity of the last of these effigies. Perhaps misled by a collective epitaph published by Millin (which referred to Louis II of Clermont "dit le Bon"), he thought that the gisant of Pierre of Bourbon (whom he sometimes termed "Philip" and whose designation as duke of Bourbon he altered to "Burgundy") might possibly represent "Louis 2 Earl of Clermont surnamed the Good who is said to be buried in the same place and died 1404."[139] Kerrich's hesitation about the identity of the monument is puzzling, for both Montfaucon and Millin (the former of whom Kerrich specifically cited on one of his sketches) repro-

---

[134] See above at notes 23–24. For the arms of Valois, *semé de France à la bordure de gueules,* see Anselme, 1: 99; the arms of Louis's mother, Mahaut of Châtillon, contained a label of azure of three points (ibid., 1: 102). For the arms of Charles of Etampes, see below.

[135] See Anselme, 1: 280.

[136] BL, Add. Ms. 6728, fols. 12, 30, 32, 35, 37. For the Gaignières drawings of the tomb, see Adhémar, "Tombeaux," no. 704 and Bodl., GD-G, 1, fols. 16, 18.

[137] BL, Add. Ms. 6728, fol. 84, no. 1; Add. Ms. 6732, fol. 51 (referring to Bonfons, *Fastes* [fol. 157]); Anselme, 1: 280; Corrozet, *Antiqvitez,* 1: fol. 85.

[138] See Table A.

[139] BL, Add. Ms. 6728, fols. 165–67. Millin published the collective epitaph for members of the Bourbon line buried at the Jacobins in *Antiquités nationales,* 4: art. XXXIX, 69; Kerrich at some point copied it (BL, Add. Ms. 6732, fol. 46). Louis II, duke of Bourbon and count of Clermont, called the Good, in fact died in 1410 and was interred in the chapel of the priory of Souvigny: Anselme, 1: 301–302; see Adhémar, "Tombeaux," nos. 1041–42 for Gaignières drawings of the tomb he shared with his wife, Anne, dauphiness of Auvergne. It was their son Louis, dead at sixteen in 1404, who was buried at the Jacobins in Paris: Anselme, 1: 302, who states that he lay in the chapel of Saint Thomas Aquinas, "sous une tombe de cuivre, autour de laquelle est son épitaphe." See Millin, *Antiquités nationales,* 4: no. XXXIX, 68, for his epitaph, and, for the Gaignières drawing of his metal tomb, Adhémar, "Tombeaux", no. 994.

duced and identified the distinctive monument as that of Pierre of Bourbon.[140] The notes on his drawings suggest, however, that in the end he came to believe that the effigy indeed represented Pierre.

Of the memorials that Kerrich drew in the early 1770s at the Cordeliers and the Jacobins, six survive today.[141] Depictions of all the funerary monuments which Kerrich sketched and engraved can be found in the Gaignières collections and in the works of Corrozet, Bonfons, Montfaucon, and Millin. Kerrich's work is nonetheless valuable, providing as it does details and descriptions found in no other surviving source.

In 1785 Kerrich executed a series of engravings based on the drawings and notes he had made in Paris. He may well have engraved all eleven of the gisants he had sketched at the Cordeliers and the Jacobins, but only seven—all depicting effigies at the Jacobins—survive, and only one was ever published.[142] Illustrating the paper on funerary monuments which he read before the Society of Antiquaries in 1814, he included the effigy of Louis of Evreux, uncle of Edward III, because, he said, "The person it represents was in some measure connected with England."[143] Kerrich remarked of Louis's tomb, "I am told it still exists, but in a mutilated state: when I made my drawings it was perfect, and had, I thought, so much merit, and was so curious that it ought to be preserved." Despite his awareness of the devastation caused by the Revolution, and despite his belief that "the history of the arts in France is totally unknown," Kerrich's article nonetheless concentrated on tombs he had seen and drawn in Italy.

Although most of Kerrich's engravings of the Parisian funerary monuments were never published, they served an exceedingly useful purpose after the antiquarian in England who undertook research for Debret discovered them. Unlike the Gaignières drawings in Oxford, the engravings could be—and were—sent to Paris. There they notably advanced the work of Debret.[144]

---

[140] Montfaucon, 2: pl. LVI, no. 1, facing 326, and 326; Millin, *Antiquités nationales,* 4: art. XXXIX, pl. X, fig. 2, facing 67, and 66–67; for Gaignières drawings of the tomb, see Adhémar, "Tombeaux," no. 800. The gisant was partially destroyed during the Revolution, but Lenoir exhibited the surviving bust in his museum before sending it to Saint-Denis: Lenoir, *Musée,* 2: 73, no. 526, and 8: 175, no. 526 (for the delivery of the piece to Saint-Denis); see also *Inventaire général des richesses,* 3: 168. It then disappeared. Guilhermy's notes on a list of monuments taken to Saint-Denis contain the query, "Pierre duc de Bourbon où est-il?": Guilhermy, BN, n.a.f. 6121, fol. 133v. A plaster cast of the bust, executed by L.-Eugène Bion in 1839, is preserved at the Musée national des Châteaux de Versailles et de Trianon, MV 572.

[141] At Saint-Denis are exhibited the two tombs from the Cordeliers, and those of Charles of Anjou, Louis of Evreux, Charles of Valois, and Charles of Alençon: Erlande-Brandenburg, *L'église abbatiale,* 2: nos. 27–28, 39–42, and idem, in Erlande-Brandenburg et al., *Le roi, la sculpture et la mort,* 17–18, 20–23. Like the equestrian statue of Philip IV at Notre-Dame, the entrail tomb of Philip VI and the monuments of Philip of Artois, Robert of Clermont, Louis of Clermont, and Pierre of Bourbon have disappeared; see the preceding note for the cast of the bust of Pierre of Bourbon at Versailles.

[142] I have found no trace of any engraving based on his numerous sketches of the equestrian statue of Notre-Dame.

[143] For this and the following quotations, see Kerrich, "Sepulchral Monuments," 193.

[144] See above at n. 47.

TABLE A

Tomb JACOBINS	Kerrich Drawings[1]	Kerrich Engraving	Other Sources[5]
1. Charles of Anjou (d. 1285)	fols. 103–4	BM,[2] 1867-3-9-557 FM,[3] fol. 7 JSM,[4] fol. 8	Adhémar, no. 450
2. Philip of Artois (d. 1298)	fols. 104–7	BM, 1861-10-12-2464 FM, fol. 13 JSM, fol. 7	Montfaucon, 2: pl. XXXVIII, no. 5, following p. 214
3. Robert of Clermont (d. 1318)	fols. 101–3 (cf. BL, Add. Ms. 6732, fols. 46, 48)	BM, 1861-10-12-2467 1931-4-13-173 FM, fol. 3 JSM, fol. 9	Adhémar, nos. 618, 723
4. Louis of Evreux (d. 1319)	fols. 98–99	BM, 1873-5-10-2673 1931-4-13-176 JSM, fol. 6	Adhémar, no. 624
5. Charles of Valois (d. 1325)	fols. 99–100	BM, 1861-10-12-2470 1931-4-13-175 FM, fol. 6 JSM, fol. 10	Adhémar, no. 657
6. Louis of Clermont (d. 1342)	fols. 108–10 (cf. BL, Add. Ms. 6732, fol. 46)	BM, 1861-10-12-2468 FM, fol. 5 JSM, fol. 11	Adhémar, nos. 723–25
7. Charles of Alençon (d. 1346)	fols. 127–28		Adhémar, no. 884
8. Philip VI (d. 1350)	fol. 126		Adhémar, nos. 763–bis
9. Pierre of Bourbon (d. 1356)	fols. 165–67	BM, 1873-5-10-2674 FM, fol. 4 JSM, fol. 5	Adhémar, no. 800

TABLE A—*Continued*

Tomb CORDELIERS	Kerrich Drawings[1]	Kerrich Engravings	Other Sources[5]
10. "Louis of Valois" (d. 1328)/Robert l'Enfant of Artois (d. 1317)	fols. 81–83		Adhémar, no. 611 Cf. Lenoir, *Musée,* 2: pl. 31, no. 25, facing p. 196
11. Charles of Etampes (d. 1336)	fols. 84–85		Adhémar, no. 704 Lenoir, *Musée,* 2: pl. 66, no. 48, facing p. 68

1. Unless otherwise specified, the references to the Kerrich drawings are to BL, Add. Ms. 6728.

2. BM, Department of Prints and Drawings. The engravings acquired in 1931 are mounted in vol. 1 of a two-volume set owned by Sir Richard Bull, "Etchings and Engravings of the Nobility and Gentry of England, or, by Persons not Exercising the Art as a Trade"; the other engravings are housed in a portfolio containing Kerrich's work.

3. Cambridge, Fitzwilliam Museum, 28-L-13, "Etchings, by Kerrich," a volume containing thirteen of Kerrich's engravings, three engravings after Kerrich by Jane C. Hayles (who did the engraved frontispiece), and one engraving by T. Stothard.

4. London, Sir John Soane's Museum and Architectural Library, Drawer No. 58, Set 5, "Sundry Antiquarian Prints, Small Monumental Effigies," containing fifteen engravings by Kerrich and three engravings after Kerrich by Jane C. Hayles.

5. No attempt is made to give all depictions of the tombs. The Gaignières drawings of the gisants are in every case given; additional sources that are cited differ significantly from or complement the Gaignières drawings.

APPENDIX III

THE DISAPPEARANCE OF THE OXFORD COLLECTION OF GAIGNIERES DRAWINGS FROM THE FRENCH ROYAL LIBRARY

Mystery has long shrouded the circumstances under which the Gaignières drawings now at Oxford left Paris and the Bibliothèque royale.[145] Debret and others believed they had been lost at the time of the Revolution.[146] Since 1862 their departure has generally been linked with the Gevigney scandal, which shook the royal library in 1784. There is no sure proof that Jean-Baptiste Guillaume de Gevigney (1729–1802), conservator of documents and genealogies at the library from 1779 to 1784, committed this particular crime—although, as his biographers have shown, he was a consummate scoundrel and an inveterate kleptomaniac and forger.[147] Suspicion that he had forged documents and stolen and sold material from the royal library led to his forced retirement in 1784. The testimony he gave under interrogation was calculated to deceive and to protect his reputation, and he was never prosecuted. Nonetheless, his curious comments on the Gaignières drawings that are now in Oxford are damning and provide convincing testimony of his guilt.

For many years Gevigney's name was shielded, first by good fortune and then, apparently, by the embarrassment occasioned by a conservator's involvement in crime. The first serious investigation of the history of the Oxford collection was conducted in 1859 by a special commission consisting of nine men, among them Léon de Laborde, Prosper Mérimée, Michel Hennin, the Baron de Guilhermy, and Albert Lenoir, all of them familiar with the Oxford drawings. Léopold Delisle, then an employee in the department of manuscripts at the Bibliothèque impériale, assisted in their

[145] I am grateful to Jean-Bernard de Vaivre for encouraging me to investigate this question, and to Marie-Noëlle Baudouin-Matuszek for her invaluable help and advice, and for references to the material in the BN which I cite. Mme. Baudouin-Matuszek and I are collaborating on a study of the Gevigney affair which we hope to publish in the near future.

[146] See above, at nn. 64 and 73.

[147] Most useful for Gevigney's life are Jules Gauthier, "Un précurseur de Libri. Etude sur le généalogiste Jean-Baptiste Guillaume de Gevigney, sa vie, son oeuvre, ses aventures et ses méfaits," *Mémoires de la Société d'émulation du Doubs* 7th ser., 6 (1901): 220–62; and Jacques Laurent, "M. de Gevigney, seigneur de Percey-le-Petit, amateur d'art," *Revue des questions historiques* 56e année, no. 2, 216e livraison (1 April 1928): 344–74. Neither utilized the dossier of judicial documents discussed below.

investigations.[148] On 26 February 1860 Charles Aimé Dauban delivered the commission's report to the Ministre de l'Instruction publique et des Cultes. The Oxford drawings, he announced, had been taken from twenty-five portfolios of drawings of monuments belonging to Roger de Gaignières, which had been delivered to the royal library on 25 September 1716 and were in the royal collection in 1760. The commission hypothesized that the royal library still had the portfolios in 1785, since in that year the abbé Coupé, recently appointed conservator of documents and genealogies, inserted marginal notes in an inventory of the Gaignières collection immediately preceding entries relating to the portfolios; the commission reasoned that Coupé would surely have commented on the disappearance of the portfolios had they been missing. Noting that a number of drawings originally in the portfolios were still at the imperial library,[149] the commission was at a loss to explain when and how the Oxford drawings had been stolen, particularly since the bindings of the fourteen bound Oxford volumes were, somewhat puzzlingly, thought to date from the reign of Louis XIV or Louis XV (1715–74)—an uncomfortably long span of time for bindings that are in any case undistinguished and had simply been described as "old."[150] Gevigney appeared in a footnote to the report simply as Coupé's predecessor; curiously, the commission confessed its inability to determine when he had left the library.[151]

Two and a half years later the puzzle was apparently solved, although Gevigney was still not implicated. On 11 June 1862 Edgard Boutaric communicated to the Société impériale des antiquaires de France his discovery of "a series of judicial documents" at the Archives impériales which, he proposed, showed how the Oxford drawings had left the royal library. He did not describe the documents precisely, but he said they demonstrated that the drawings were still at the library in 1781 and had been stolen between 1781 and 1784 "par une personne préposée à leur garde." As proof he cited "un fragment d'interrogatoire" dated 28 September 1784, containing questions and answers relating to a number of manuscripts the suspect was accused of stealing. Boutaric quoted most of two interchanges. The first involved a volume entitled *Epitaphes des églises de Picardie,* which had been in the library in June 1781; of the book the suspect said he knew nothing. He was also asked about some large portfolios from the

[148] On Delisle's career at the library, see Georges Perrot, "Notice sur la vie et les travaux de Léopold-Victor Delisle," *Bibliothèque de l'Ecole des Chartes* 73 (1912): 5–72, at 16–20, 25–28; and E.-G. Ledos, "M. Léopold Delisle et la Bibliothèque nationale," *Revue des bibliothèques* 37 (1927): 116–51.

[149] The commission focused particularly on the portfolios of drawings from Normandy: Dauban, "Rapport," 173–74. Those which remained in Paris are now in BN, RE, Pe 8.

[150] Dauban, "Rapport," 165, 171–75. The commission's reasoning is difficult to fathom. The portfolios were not bound when Gaignières died on 27 March 1715, just five months before Louis XIV. De Laborde and Mérimée had seen the volumes when they were in Oxford in 1850, but their appraisal of the bindings is unrecorded; Alfred Hackman apparently informed Michel Hennin simply that they were bound "d'une reliure ancienne": ibid., 170, n. 1, and see above, at nn. 80 and 90.

[151] Dauban, "Rapport," 174, n. 1.

Gaignières collection bearing the names of different French provinces, one of them *Isle de France,* which consisted of drawings of burial sites and tombs of ecclesiastical and lay lords and copies of their epitaphs, and which had been kept in a screened cabinet in the second room of the department of documents and genealogies. The suspect replied that most of the drawings had been spoiled and filled with worms, that those which could be saved had been filed with material related to armorial bearings and genealogies or had been given to Bignon, the head of the library, for the Cabinet des estampes; the rest had been thrown out. Boutaric concluded that these items were the volumes which had subsequently been deposited at Oxford after having passed through the hands of different English collectors.[152] Boutaric was eminently—and frustratingly—discreet. He said nothing of Richard Gough; he did not give the documents' class mark; he did not mention the identity of the man who had been questioned (in fact Jean-Baptiste Guillaume de Gevigney); he gave no hint of the outcome of the interrogation. Further, his reference to the volume of epitaphs was misleading, since no such volume exists at Oxford, nor was it identified with the Gaignières collection; there is thus no reason why the Gaignières portfolios could not have been taken before June 1781. Despite its limitations, Boutaric's report exercised considerable influence over his contemporaries, and particularly Léopold Delisle, who in 1868, two years after being named librarian of the department of manuscripts, published the first volume of his history of the Cabinet des manuscrits.[153]

Delisle had been responsible for the meticulous research underlying the report presented by Dauban in 1860, but he did not pursue the investigation Boutaric had begun. The account of the theft of the Gaignières drawings which he presented in 1868 relied solely on Boutaric's short notice—rather than his source. In Delisle's book Gevigney figures not as a suspected or known thief, but rather as the donor in 1772 and 1773 of original documents concerning Burgundy, Lorraine, and the Barrois, and as the abbé de La Cour's successor as conservator of documents and genealogies from 1779 to 1784. Simply citing Boutaric's account and declaring it "selon toute apparence" reliable, Delisle said that while Gevigney was in office, "un malfaiteur" had taken various Gaignières volumes from the royal collection, and because of this "grand malheur" Gevigney had been forced to leave his post. Delisle mentioned no other losses; he said nothing of Gevigney's earlier or later career, aside from remarking that a collection of documents which he amassed had passed to the Archives départementales

[152] Boutaric, *Bulletin de la Société impériale des antiquaires de France* (1862): 85–86. For the volume of epitaphs of Picardy, see n. 186 below.

[153] Delisle commented on the progress of his work on the book in letters to Henry d'Arbois de Jubainville on 21 July 1868 (when both the first and second volumes were virtually finished), 11 September 1868, and 31 October 1878 (when he was trying to complete the third): *Lettres de Léopold Delisle,* ed. Xavier Delisle, fasc. 5, *Correspondance adressée à Henry d'Arbois de Jubainville, 1852–1909* (Bar-le-Duc: Contant-Laguerre, 1913), 137–39, nos. CXV and CXVI, and 195–96, no. CLXIV.

de la Côte-d'Or.[154] The third volume of Delisle's history was published in 1881, seven years after he had become head of the national library. In the additions and corrections contained in this volume, Delisle did not fully reveal the suspicions regarding Gevigney that had been aroused since 1868, although he did cite two adverse judgments concerning Gevigney. The first was given by the same Dauban who had presented the report in 1860 and whose book on Parisian prisons, published in 1870, had, Delisle said, charged Gevigney with procuring documents for Caron de Beaumarchais; in the first volume of his history Delisle had noted Beaumarchais' sale to the library "in 1784 or 1785" of numerous documents from the Chambre des comptes, but neither in 1868 nor in 1881 did he otherwise allude to Beaumarchais' ties to Gevigney.[155] The second criticism of Gevigney which Delisle cited was that of Barthélemy Mercier, abbot of Saint-Léger, who, according to Delisle, had accused Gevigney of robbing the royal library and, before fleeing, giving his loot to a type-founder to whom he was indebted, who had in turn sold the volumes of genealogies to Dom Brial for 24 l. Delisle himself advanced no judgment, nor did he indicate that the documentation on which Dauban drew was the same dossier to which Boutaric had called attention or that Dauban charged Gevigney with stealing the Oxford drawings.[156] Rather, he concentrated on the less damning ties between Gevigney and Beaumarchais which Dauban revealed. Delisle ended by referring again to Gevigney's own collection of documents (here called "fort importants"), then in the archives of the Côte-d'Or.[157] Even when in 1890 Delisle himself unmasked one of Gevigney's most egregious forgeries, he refrained from connecting the conservator explicitly with the theft of the Gaignières volumes, although he again quoted Mercier's condemnation of Gevigney. Delisle concluded, "La moralité de Guillaume est donc suffisamment établie," and declared him guilty of forging the diploma of 1218 under examination.[158]

Delisle prided himself on his judiciousness and caution, but he was also dedicated to the pursuit of truth, and he spent much time and effort

---

[154] Delisle, *Cabinet des manuscrits*, 1: 554, 556.

[155] Delisle, *Cabinet des manuscrits*, 1: 551, 2: 287.

[156] Charles Aimé Dauban, *Les prisons de Paris sous la Révolution d'après les relations des contemporains, avec des notes et une introduction* (Paris: Henri Plon, 1870), 31–33, where, discussing "la moralité de Beaumarchais," Dauban pays considerable attention to Gevigney, who he says took from the royal library and gave or sold to Beaumarchais the many documents that were eventually seized and taken to the library. He does not note that Gevigney betrayed Beaumarchais, but he presents Gevigney as unscrupulously exploiting his position to line his own pockets; quoting Gevigney's response to the question concerning the Gaignières portfolios, he blames Gevigney for their theft. Dauban does not refer to the class mark of the judicial documents he used, although he gives the names of the commissioner, Chénon, who carried out the investigation, and of the lieutenant general of police, Le Noir, who ordered it; he was apparently unaware that Le Noir had succeeded Bignon as head of the library.

[157] Delisle, *Cabinet des manuscrits*, 3: 375.

[158] Léopold Delisle, "Un faux diplôme de l'empereur Frédéric II (16 mars 1218)," in his *Littérature latine et histoire du Moyen Age* (Instructions du Comité des Travaux historiques; Paris: Imprimerie nationale, 1890), 52–59. For comments on Delisle's stance, see Laurent, "M. de Gevigney," 347.

remedying the omissions and errors he freely acknowledged existed in his history of the library.[159] He was implacable in unmasking those who had despoiled the Bibliothèque nationale, denounced them with righteous indignation, and sought to recover what they had taken.[160] It is difficult to say why he did not investigate more fully the disappearance of the Gaignières volumes and the affair of Gevigney, who had been accused of stealing much more than these portfolios from the library. He was perhaps reluctant to accuse a man whose guilt was not fully established, but there is no evidence that he attempted to establish whether or not Gevigney had committed the crime. He was doubtless loath to admit that a man who had been a conservator of the royal library, the library to which he had devoted his own life, had betrayed the trust with which he had been charged; he expected all who worked at the library to serve with the same selfless dedication as did he.[161] Whatever the explanation, in this instance Delisle avoided confronting an unpleasant truth. Not only did he use Dauban's book with curious selectiveness; never does he appear to have cited the article on Gaignières published by Georges Duplessis in 1870, an article which contained more extensive extracts from Boutaric's documents, gave the dossier's class mark, unmasked Gevigney as the man who had been interrogated about the Gaignières portfolios in 1784, and clearly indicated that he was responsible for the disappearance of the Oxford drawings.[162] The dossier of judicial documents was at this point known to many of Delisle's contemporaries, and in 1873 Arthur de Boislisle cited it for information regarding documents from the Chambre des comptes which both Gevigney and Beaumarchais possessed.[163]

Duplessis and Dauban believed that Gevigney was heavily implicated in

---

[159] Georges Espinas, "Notice nécrologique sur Léopold Delisle, membre de l'Institut, membre honoraire de la Société nationale des antiquaires de France," *Bulletin de la Société nationale des antiquaires de France* (1912): 121–75, at 135; Perrot, "Delisle," 70–72; E. Müller, "Les dernières paroles de M. Léopold Delisle recueillies par Le Chanoine E. Müller, le 22 juillet 1910," *Bulletin du bibliophile et du bibliothécaire* 8–9 (15 August–15 September 1910): 347–51, at 350; *Lettres de Delisle,* fasc. 3, *Correspondance adressée á M. le Chanoine Ulysse Chevalier, 1866–1910* (Valence: Imprimerie Valentinoise, 1912), 27, no. XXII (17 April 1880); Léopold Delisle, "Souvenirs de jeunesse," in idem, *Recherches sur la librairie de Charles V,* 2 vols. (Paris: H. Champion, 1907): 1: xxvi–vii.

[160] Ledos, "Delisle," 123–24, 144–46; Delisle, *Cabinet des manuscrits,* 1: 432, 2: 300, 304–5; idem, "Observations sur l'origine de plusieurs manuscrits de la collection de M. Barrois," *Bibliothèque de l'Ecole des Chartes* 6th ser., 2 (1886): 193–264, at 194–95; idem, *Bibliothèque nationale. Catalogue des manuscrits des fonds Libri et Barrois* (Paris: H. Champion, 1888), v–lxxxii.

[161] Delisle, *Recherches,* 1: xxiv; Espinas, "Delisle," 129, 133–34; Ledos, "Delisle," 148–49; Perrot, "Delisle," 28, 34.

[162] Duplessis, "Gaignières," 484–86, n. 1. Duplessis cited the dossier of documents as "Archives de l'Empire, section judiciaire, Y. 11427." When he examined them, the documents were indeed in this bundle, which contains the papers of Pierre Chénon, père, royal commissioner of the Châtelet, for the first half of 1785. The dossier was subsequently removed and placed with the papers in AN, Y 11425, where, chronologically, it belongs. I am grateful to Jean-Bernard de Vaivre for emphasizing to me the importance of Duplessis' article, and to Marie-Noëlle Baudouin-Matuszek and Henri Gerbaud for assisting me in locating the dossier.

[163] Arthur de Boislisle, *Chambre des comptes de Paris. Pièces justificatives pour servir á l'histoire des premiers présidents (1506–1791) . . . Notice préliminaire* (Nogent-le-Rotrou: A. Gouverneur, 1873), cxxix, where he gives the class mark of the dossier as Y 11427.

the theft of the Oxford drawings, and Gevigney's later biographers have concurred that he was responsible for the theft of the Oxford volumes. Unfamiliar with the dossier found by Boutaric, they present him, dramatically and misleadingly, as fleeing from Paris after he became a prime suspect and after a criminal investigation was launched at the Châtelet.[164]

Other scholars have been less sure of Gevigney's guilt. In the introduction to his inventory of Gaignières drawings, published in 1891, Henri Bouchot termed the theft of the volumes "le vol Gevigney" and declared Gevigney ultimately responsible for it, but he cautioned that the documents discovered by Boutaric and cited by Duplessis had not completely illuminated the affair and hesitated to say that Gevigney himself had made off with the Oxford drawings. The actual name of the culprit was in his opinion unimportant; following in the steps of the commission of 1860 he emphasized that the thief had not removed all the drawings from every portfolio.[165] The article on Gaignières which Charles de Grandmaison published in 1891 was also hesitant. Grandmaison held that part of the Gaignières collection had indeed been stolen "vers 1780," but he thought that the Oxford volumes had probably disappeared much earlier. He did not explain his reasoning, simply remarking that they were not among the Gaignières volumes which were taken to Louis XIV at Marly in June 1715. This fact, however, scarcely proved that the Oxford drawings had already been stolen. As Grandmaison himself showed, the twelve large volumes of drawings which were sent to Marly depicted costumes of various times and places, and they were intended to amuse the ailing king, who was to die on 1 September 1715.[166] Portrayals of funerary monuments would hardly have been thought suitable to distract a man who was on the verge of death. More important, as the report of 1860 had shown, the Gaignières portfolios in question were delivered to the royal library in 1716 and were there as late as 1760.

The questions raised by Bouchot and those implicit in Dauban's report have not yet been resolved, largely because the dossier of judicial documents which Boutaric discovered has never been carefully analyzed or related to Gevigney's career and to other documentation regarding the affair.[167]

---

[164] Gauthier, "Gevigney," 238; followed by Laurent, "M. de Gevigney," 353 (where he says that Gevigney faced being condemned to the galleys); and by H. Tribout de Morembert in his article on Gevigney in *Dictionnaire de biographie française*, ed. M. Prevost, Roman d'Amat, and H. Tribout de Morembert, fasc. 90 (Paris: Letouzey et Ané, 1982): 1416–18.

[165] Bouchot, 1: xx–xxi; the collection of drawings concerning Maine which Bouchot examined were unbound when they passed from Gough's hands to the Bodleian (see Appendix I). See also Dauban, "Rapport," 173–74, which Bouchot does not cite.

[166] Grandmaison, "Gaignières," (1891): 214, 216. Clairambault may have retained some of these drawings of costumes for himself: see Duplessis, "Gaignières," 481–82, n. 1, for 1182 drawings of costumes, in five volumes, which were purchased for the royal library when Clairambault's collection was sold in 1755, although note that one inventory indicates that the drawings were copies of Gaignières drawings, rather than originals.

[167] AN, Y 11425. The dossier of documents preserved by Commissioner Chénon contains twenty-eight items, ranging in date from 15 September 1784 to 20 January 1792. They are unnumbered, unpaginated, and are arranged in neither chronological nor logical order. Most concern the Gevigney and Beaumarchais affairs, but seven illuminate the difficulties which Chénon experienced in attempting to recover the money he had spent in carrying out the

In 1761 Gevigney, then thirty-two, came to Paris from his native Besançon. In Franche-Comté he had used his scholarly skills and religious vocation to gain access to numerous archives and a princely patron, Louis de Bauffremont, as well as admission to the Académie des Sciences et Belles-Lettres of Besançon. Theft and forgery had enabled him to enrich his own collection of documents and elevate the lineages of his patron and other Burgundian families. In the two years following his arrival in Paris gifts of charters to the royal library (doubtless loot acquired in Burgundy) helped him establish himself in the capital. In 1773 he was named *généalogiste des maisons et écuries de Monsieur et du comte d'Artois* and obtained the succession of the post of conservator of documents and genealogies at the royal library, where he became the deputy (*adjoint*) of the current conservator, the abbé de La Cour. De La Cour died on 7 April 1779, but Gevigney, who had many enemies, had difficulty obtaining his post. Gevigney was a shrewd manipulator, however, and after three or four months his opponents were forced to yield. His salary and perquisites, amounting to 3500 l. a year, did not alleviate the financial problems that had caused him, on 18 May 1769, to sell many of the art objects he possessed, and a larger, public sale was held in December 1779. He did not dispose of everything he had; after the sale he estimated that the paintings he retained were worth 110,961 l. and his furniture and plate 23,962 l.[168] Given his tastes and his thirst for collecting, he perennially needed cash.

Gevigney was more interested in acquiring documents for himself, many of them from the Chambre des comptes, than in swelling the royal library's holdings. There seems little question that, early on, he was suspected of enriching his own collection with documents and manuscripts from the royal library[169] or that Claude Aubron, second in command in the department of titles and genealogies, kept careful watch over the activities of the man whose position he himself had hoped to occupy.[170]

---

investigation, which he did not receive until 1792. The lengthiest piece is the detailed account of Chénon's proceedings from 16 September 1784 through 25 May 1785. The archives of the Département des manuscrits at the BN (particularly nos. 46 and 66) contain additional information, as does BN, fr. 33154.

[168] Laurent, "M. de Gevigney," 358, 372–74. As Laurent shows, the register of possessions and transactions which Gevigney kept between 1769 and 1786 (now at the Bibliothèque publique de Dijon) contains inventories prepared in 1773 and 1776 as well as 1769, which suggests that Gevigney may have contemplated additional sales in those years: ibid., 344, 358.

[169] A. Vidier, "Le Noir, bibliothécaire du roi (1784–1790). Ses démêlés avec Carra," *Bulletin de la Société de l'histoire de Paris et de l'Ile-de-France* 51 (1924): 49–61, at 51 (reflections on the state of the royal library in 1784, recorded between 1804 and Le Noir's death on 17 November 1807); but cf. Fernand Bournon, "Documents relatifs à la Bibliothèque du roi (1777–1791)," *La correspondance historique et archéologique* 15 (1908): 85–86 (a letter of Le Noir written on 16 April 1784, immediately after his appointment as head of the library, in which he comments on the misunderstanding and jealousy among the heads of the departments, signals the abuses found particularly in the department of printed books, but says nothing of the department of documents and genealogies).

[170] BN, Archives du Département des manuscrits, no. 66, fol. 83 (a letter of Aubron to the Baron de Breteuil, written shortly after Gevigney's disgrace); fol. 132 (questions to be posed to Gevigney regarding four missing documents which Aubron had copied on 10 July 1784 and Gevigney had taken three days later). For Gevigney's accusations against Aubron, at least partly substantiated by these two documents, see AN, Y 11425, interrogatory of 23 September 1784, [pp. 8, 15, 22–23].

The ax fell in September 1784, when Jean-Charles-Pierre Le Noir, lieutenant general of police in Paris and recently named head of the royal library, ordered Pierre Chénon, commissioner of the Châtelet for the district of the Louvre, to take action against Gevigney. Chénon commenced operations at 3 P.M. on Friday, 16 September, visiting Gevigney at his lodgings on the quai de la Mégisserie and searching his apartment for books and papers; some were immediately taken to the royal library, the rest placed under seal. Before the officials left, Gevigney denounced Caron de Beaumarchais, who, he said, had in storage a vast quantity of documents of the Chambre des comptes, and Chénon proceeded to sequester these hoards as well.[171] By 23 September Gevigney was being referred to as former (*cy-devant*) guardian of the department of documents and genealogies.[172] On that day Chénon formally questioned him. Among many specific items about which Chénon asked was a manuscript inventory of the Gaignières collection, and a leather portfolio and green box from the collection which Gevigney's servant had taken to his lodgings on 23 May 1782. Gevigney brazenly parried all accusations, saying that, as was customary and licit, he had been working on the documents and books he had in his lodgings, that he had no recollection of the items that were mentioned, that the only documents of which he had ever disposed were those rejected for the library. He indignantly denied ever having forged.[173] There was no escaping the fact that numerous volumes and documents were found in his lodgings. These were transported to the royal library on Monday, 27 September,[174] eleven days after Gevigney's first encounter with the authorities, four days after his first official interrogation and the day before the second. On 28 September Gevigney was questioned about many additional items, including three associated with Gaignières: an armorial from his collection, a portfolio labeled "Legitimation ou Naturalités" containing extracts by Gaignières, and, finally, the large portfolios bearing names of different provinces which, according to Chénon, Gevigney had once said he had surrendered to M. Joly, the conservator of the department of engravings.[175] Gevigney steadfastly maintained his innocence—and continued to receive his salary. On 29 October, however, he was replaced by the abbé Coupé.[176] Some five weeks later, in response to orders which Le Noir issued on 6 December 1784, Chénon began sorting and inventorying all that had been taken from Gevigney's lodgings. This process continued until 15 January, when a formal list of material belonging to the library was presented; among the documents and volumes were

---

171 AN, Y 11425, letter of Le Noir to Chénon dated 15 September 1784; *procès-verbal* of 16 September 1784–25 May 1785, [pp. 1–4].

172 AN, Y 11425, interrogatory of 23 September 1784, [p. 1].

173 AN, Y 11425, interrogatory of 23 September 1784, [pp. 14, 16]; Duplessis, "Gaignières," 485, n. 1 continued from 484.

174 AN, Y 11425, *procès-verbal* of 16 September 1784–25 May 1785, [p. 8].

175 AN, Y 11425, interrogatory of 28 September 1784, [pp. 1–3]; Duplessis, "Gaignières," 485–86, n. 1 continued from 484.

176 Bournon, "Documents," 88.

some written by Gaignières. The library claimed some 216 items, a small portion of Gevigney's collection, which also included 131,000 *quittances*, 1710 acts, 13,133 documents from the Chambre des comptes of Blois, and 33 parchment rolls consisting of 226 membranes.[177] These findings put an end to the proceedings against Gevigney, and some months passed before anything was done about Beaumarchais' documents.

Gevigney had refused to admit his guilt, and the authorities may have concluded that it would be difficult to convict him. His salary did not end until 28 October 1784, termed the day of his retirement (*retraite*), and although Le Noir acknowledged in his annual report on the library that under Gevigney his department had been neglected and even robbed (*pillé*) and that Gevigney had been dismissed (*remercié*), he did not charge Gevigney with theft.[178] Le Noir's ties to Beaumarchais may also have helped protect Gevigney, since, however much he had denied it, Gevigney was clearly in a position to inflict further damage on Beaumarchais' reputation.[179] In all likelihood Gevigney agreed to abandon all the documents that had been seized in return for freedom from prosecution. As one of his biographers suggests, he may also have had an influential patron or accomplice who intervened for him.[180] It is difficult to believe that flight and hiding enabled him to escape the arm of the law.

Gevigney was clever; he was a survivor. By October 1786 he was back in Burgundy, making extensive repairs on the house he owned at Percey-le-Petit. He does not seem to have feared prosecution, and in 1789 he appeared at the assembly of nobles of the *bailliage* of Langres. Gevigney was too shrewd to flaunt his claims to nobility during the Revolution, and he married, had children, and lived as a bourgeois and municipal administrator in Dijon. Nonetheless, unable to renounce his old habits, he seems to have profited from the turmoil of the times to collect numerous documents which eventually enriched the collection of the Baron de Joursanvault—and his own. At his death on 8 September 1802 he left his widow a huge, disordered legacy of documents, many of which were sold, by weight, to the departmental archives of the Côte-d'Or.[181]

So much for Gevigney's life. He clearly had the opportunity to take the Gaignières drawings; he needed the money he could obtain by selling

---

[177] AN, Y 11425, *procès-verbal* of 16 September 1784–25 May 1785, [pp. 8–29]; letter of Le Noir to Chénon dated 6 December 1784.

[178] Bournon, "Documents," 88, 93.

[179] For Le Noir's ties to Beaumarchais, see BN, Archives du Département des manuscrits, no. 66, fol. 153 (a note apparently written on 19 March 1785 which refers to Le Noir as Beaumarchais' friend); [Jean-Louis Carra], *L'an 1787. Précis de l'administration de la Bibliothèque du roi, sous M. Lenoir . . .*, 2nd ed. (Liège: no pub., 1788), 10–11. See AN, Y 11425, interrogatory of 23 September 1784, [p. 19–20], for Gevigney's ineffective attempts to deny acquaintance and traffic with Beaumarchais.

[180] Tribout de Morembert, in *Dictionnaire de biographie française*, fasc. 90 (1982): 1418.

[181] Laurent, "M. de Gevigney," 345–47, 353–57. For the fate of his collection, see C.-H. Maillard de Chambure, *Rapport à M. le Ministre de l'Instruction publique, sur le Cabinet de chartes de M. de Gevigney, acquis pour les Archives générales de Bourgogne et du département de la Côte-d'Or* (Beaune: Blondeau-Dejussieu, 1859).

them; only fear of compromising his position would have deterred him from theft. But was it actually he who took the Oxford drawings? The answer to this question lies, I believe, in Gevigney's lengthy and apologetic testimony concerning the Gaignières portfolios, evidence that deserves closer examination than it has received.

On 23 and 28 September 1784 Gevigney responded briefly and evasively to most of the questions he was asked. Of the manuscript inventory of the Gaignières collection he said that it was in the library; he said the same of the leather portfolio and green box, which he claimed he had "probably" returned to the library. According to him, the Gaignières armorial of Auvergne, Bourbonnais, and Forez had been taken back to the library, and it was indeed there on 7 December 1784.[182] The Gaignières portfolio concerning legitimation, Gevigney said, was also at the library, and it too was accounted for on 18 June 1785.[183] These responses were typical. Gevigney repeatedly claimed that items had never been removed from the library or had been returned, that he had no knowledge of them, or that others had taken them. His testimony concerning the Gaignières provincial portfolios is strikingly different. In only one other case, involving original documents of Charles d'Hozier, did Gevigney make a similar response, claiming that the documents in question had indeed been inventoried before being distributed to different locations or jettisoned.[184] Likewise, in the case of the Gaignières portfolios Gevigney did not deny that he knew and had used them.[185] As has been seen, he claimed that they had been winnowed out and all that were well-preserved divided between

---

[182] AN, Y 11425, *procès-verbal* of 16 September 1784–25 May 1785, [p. 9]; the Armorial is not listed among those items received by the abbé Coupé on 18 June 1785, perhaps because its presence at the library had already been confirmed: see BN, fr. 33154, fol. 90.

[183] BN, fr. 33154, fol. 90.

[184] On 23 September 1784 Gevigney was asked "S'il n'est pas vrai qu'il a encore soustrait plusieurs titres originaux de la main du Sieur Charles Dhozier qui avoient eté mis a part lors qu'on fit la verification de son cabinet en 1780. parce que l'inventaire n'en faisoit pas mention"; he responded "que ces titres doivent se trouver rapportés a la fin de l'inventaire sommaire, fait par le repondant de la Biblioteque, et qu'ils ont eté distribués, ou dans les boëtes ou dans les supplemens, ou mis au nombre des titres rebutés." See AN, Y 11425, interrogatory of 23 September 1784, [p. 12]. Five days later Chénon questioned Gevigney again about this item: "Que sont devenus des titres en parchemin qui se trouvoient parmi les pieces non inventoriées qui ont eté retirés des boetes du cabinet de Mr. D'Hozier lors du recollement qui en a eté fait en 1779 depuis." In response Gevigney simply referred to his previous answer. See AN, Y 11425, interrogatory of 28 September 1783, [p. 3].

[185] Chénon's question was the following: "Des Porte feüilles grands in folio du même cabinet cottés des noms de differentes provinces et dont l'vn etoit cotté *Isle de France:* ils contenoient des dessins à la plume, d'anciens mausolés et tombeaux de seigneurs tant ecclesiastiques que laïcs et les copies de leurs epitaphes.

Ces porte feüilles etoient placés dans le cabinet grillé de la seconde salle du depot.

Mr. De Gevigney les a til remis a Mr. Joly comme il l'a dit dans le tems." Gevigney responded, "La pluspart de ces feüilles etoient pourries et remplies de vers. on a extrait ce qui pouvoit être conservé, et on les a inserées dans des cartons d'armoiries, et de genealogies, d'autres ont eté remis a Mr. Bignon pour les remettre au cabinet des Estampes—

Le surplus a eté abandonné comme pourri—": AN, Y 11425, interrogatory of 23 September 1784 [pp. 2–3]; cf. Boutaric, *Bulletin de la Société impériale des antiquaires de France* (1862): 86; and Duplessis, "Gaignières," 486, n. 1 continued from 484.

his department and the Cabinet des estampes. In this case he surely protested too much, although his answer may well have forestalled suspicion. To answer the question posed in Dauban's report, the abbé Coupé would scarcely have bothered to note the absence of portfolios which were commonly believed no longer to exist.[186]

Gevigney's assertion that most of the drawings in the portfolios were spoiled and worm-eaten and that many had been jettisoned gives the lie to his testimony. The drawings that have survived are in excellent condition, and the research that resulted in Dauban's report of 1860, confirmed by the findings of Bouchot, reveal how few of the drawings recorded in the early inventories of the Gaignières collection are missing.

The conclusion seems clear. The portfolios had been in Gevigney's hands. Perhaps at some point he talked to Joly, conservator of the Cabinet des estampes, about depositing them in that department. To cover his tracks, he extracted a number of the drawings, placing some elsewhere in his own department and giving others to Bignon for the Cabinet des estampes. The rest, it seems clear, he disposed of for his own benefit; he may well have had most of them bound before selling them. Had Gevigney not been guilty, he would have responded less directly to Chénon's question and refrained from fabricating the patently fictitious story he related on 28 September 1784.

[186] There is no reference to the portfolios in the lists of items enumerated on 18 June 1785 as recovered by and missing from the library, BN, fr. 33154, fols. 90–92. The lists admittedly omit many items about which Gevigney was questioned and include others which were not mentioned. The volume of epitaphs of Picardy signaled by Boutaric was listed as still missing: ibid., fol. 92.

INDEX

PUBLICATIONS

OF

The American Philosophical Society

The publications of the American Philosophical Society consist of PROCEEDINGS, TRANSACTIONS, MEMOIRS, and YEAR BOOK.

THE PROCEEDINGS contains papers which have been read before the Society in addition to other papers which have been accepted for publication by the Committee on Publications. In accordance with the present policy one volume is issued each year, consisting of four quarterly numbers, and the price is $24.00 net per volume. Individual copies may be purchased at $10.00 per copy.

THE TRANSACTIONS, the oldest scholarly journal in America, was started in 1769. In accordance with the present policy each annual volume is a collection of monographs, each issued as a part. The current annual subscription price is $70.00 net per volume. Individual copies of the TRANSACTIONS are offered for sale.

Each volume of the MEMOIRS is published as a book. The titles cover the various fields of learning; most of the recent volumes have been historical. The price of each volume is determined by its size and character, but subscribers are offered a 20 per cent discount.

The YEAR BOOK is of considerable interest to scholars because of the reports on grants for research and to libraries for this reason and because of the section dealing with the acquisitions of the Library. In addition it contains the Charter and Laws, and lists of members, and reports of committees and meetings. The YEAR BOOK is published about April 1 for the preceding calendar year. The current price is $12.00. A separate volume of GRANTEES' REPORTS is published annually. The listed price is $10.00.

An author desiring to submit a manuscript for publication should send it to the Editor, American Philosophical Society, 104 South Fifth Street, Philadelphia, Pa. 19106.

www.ingramcontent.com/pod-product-compliance
Lightning Source LLC
LaVergne TN
LVHW081603100826
845153LV00004B/448

9780871697851